D1242397

ALSO BY DARRELL KEEZER

37 Ways Your Website Died and How to Resurrect It

Darrell Keezer

PICK UP YOUR FREAKIN' PHONE

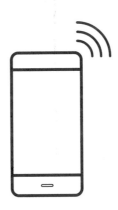

The new rules for entrepreneurs

DARRELL KEEZER

ISBN 978-0-9939457-2-4 (paperback)
ISBN 978-0-9939457-3-1 (ebook)

Also available as an audiobook: ISBN 978-0-9939457-4-8

Published by Candybox Marketing Inc.
Printed in Canada

To order books, go to www.pickupyourfreakinphone.com

Book producer and editor   Tracy Bordian/AtLargeEditorial.com
Cover design   Ben Reimer
Interior design   Susan Macgregor
Page layout   Rob Scanlan/First Image
Proofreading   Eleanor Gasparik and Heather From
Indexing   Karen Hunter

For more information, visit **www.pickupyourfreakinphone.com**

For marketing and publicity inquiries, please contact
hello@candyboxmarketing.com

www.candyboxmarketing.com

I'm often asked what motivates me to get up in the morning, and my response is always the same: four kids who crawl all over me in bed asking for food. This book is dedicated to my four little munchkins who are always a light in my life.

CONTENTS

PREFACE

In 2008 I was laid off from my job with just $8,000 of severance in my bank account. Today I run a multimillion-dollar online marketing company that has grown by 50% every year for the past 5 years. I've never received any investor dollars, taken out a loan, or carried a credit card balance. But you need to understand that this success didn't happen overnight. It didn't happen because I had one good idea. It took a lot of learning and failing, and a relentless desire to build something awesome.

In the past few years I've been fortunate enough to win a few awards for entrepreneurship, and I am humbled to find myself being recognized on the international stage (although I sometimes still feel like a junior who is just getting started with a few good wins under my belt). As a millennial who has built what many would consider a successful company in a short amount of time and with very limited resources, I am also constantly asked for my opinion about how to start a business, from the initial launch to finding that first customer to establishing a business structure. This book is my best attempt to answer some of those questions.

Anyone can start a business. You walk dogs in exchange for money? That's a business. You design logos and sell them to your network? That's a business. You get your licence to sell homes and work independently as an agent? That's a business. All of these ventures are incredible training grounds for people who want to dip a toe into entrepreneurship, but make no mistake: These types of enterprises are not companies.

A company is a group of people who gather around a business idea and collectively aim to fill or create (and fill) customers' needs. *A company of people.* This distinction is important because many people talk about starting a company when, in fact, all they want is to establish a business to exercise their trade. Entrepreneurs are people who start *and* gather people around a central idea, and good entrepreneurs make sure they are not needed to complete the work.

There is nothing wrong with wanting to own your own business and not build a company, but it's important to recognize which of these options you are choosing right from the beginning because the distinction will guide you in every single decision that you'll make. If you are going it alone, you don't need to establish building blocks beyond yourself. You can surround yourself with every task, system, and process that works *for you* because you are going to be running it going forward. If you are building a company — even if you haven't hired a ton of people yet — you will build it for a group of people to take over.

Starting a company is not for the faint of heart. I know from experience that it's as wonderful as it is painful at times. Over the past 10 years I have started many companies — some wildly successful, some beautiful failures — and I've loved every minute of it.

Although this book can help people who are starting either a business or a company, I'm writing it specifically for entrepreneurs who want to start and grow a business beyond themselves. It's for people who have their sights set on big things, not simply getting paid for their time. It's for people who will devote years of pain for long-term gain.

I hope you enjoy the read.

Darrell Keezer
October 2018

IT'S NEVER A GOOD TIME TO START A BUSINESS

Week one of starting my own business was behind me. I was at home when my phone rang: A family member was calling to ask if I needed money for groceries. Seriously. I didn't even know what to say, but I could tell that they were concerned for my young family's well-being.

You see, I had just been laid off from my job as a project manager during the "great recession" of 2008. I was newly married, had a one-year-old baby (Grace), and my wife was six months pregnant with our second daughter (Claire). We lived in a small townhouse and had recently put down a deposit on a new home for our growing family. After losing my job, we could no longer afford the home we had just sold let alone the bigger home we wanted to buy. What the heck was I thinking starting a business?

Bear with me here and I'll explain.

The truth is, it's *never* a good time to start a business. People are always waiting for the conditions to be perfect before they make the leap. Any of the following sound familiar?

I'm waiting until I have enough money to go out on my own.

I'm waiting for the perfect time to leave my job.

I'm waiting to have enough time to start something.

I'm waiting for the right opportunity to present itself.

Let me tell you, I've never met anyone who started their own business under perfect conditions. People who wait for perfection will most likely go to their grave wondering if they could have ever made it. I'm not saying that you should throw caution to the wind and ignore your circumstances, but it's not like responding to a job posting. You don't just apply to become an entrepreneur and wait for someone else to approve your situation. You need to make it happen.

You may never have enough money to start a business, but there are many ways to start with little (or no) money. See Chapter 3, where I outline how to find startup customers instead of startup capital.

There may never be a perfect time to exit your job, but are you going to let that hold you back? You've picked up this book (thanks!), and I believe it contains enough information to get you started on *something*, even if it's small at first. Chapter 2 runs through all of the items you'll need to check off your list during your first week in business.

You will never have enough spare time to start something on the side. Starting up a successful new company requires dedication and focus. See Chapter 8, where I show you how to own your calendar.

Conditions for starting a company will never be perfect, easy, or straightforward — starting a company is inherently messy — but if you are willing to take one of the biggest risks in your life, I think you'll find it's one of the most satisfying leaps you'll ever make.

My Very Early Years

Let's back up so I can explain what led up to my decision to start a digital marketing agency with almost no money in the middle of a recession. The idea didn't occur to me overnight. It started in my mind/heart/soul years before I lost my job. It seemed to poke its head out whenever I considered what I wanted to do for a living. In fact, my fascination with starting companies began at a very young age.

When I was 6 years old I was given a school project to grow a plant. I chose a sunflower. Water is the plant's food, I was told, and so I walked home for lunch (in the good ol' days when that was allowed) and hosed down that flower every flippin' day until it was 8 feet tall. I wanted it to grow big.

I wasn't interested in having the tallest plant, though. I was interested in what happened when it got big. I was told that it would produce sunflower seeds, and it occurred to me that was something I could sell to make money. After I cut that monster flower down, I

YOU NEED TO HAVE AN INTERNAL DRIVE TO SUCCESSFULLY START A COMPANY.

counted over 2,100 seeds and divided them into little baggies. Then I grabbed a piece of paper and made a sign: "Buy FREE Sunflower Seeds."

I figured I had to include the word *free* somewhere. TV and print advertising always seemed to offer *free* stuff. After a little advice from my mother, who informed me that I wouldn't make any money selling seeds for free, I decided to price them at $1 a bag.

That was it. I was off to sell those seeds door to door. Who wouldn't say yes to a little white-haired 4-year-old with his red wagon? It was the best summer of my life. Selling a product was the most exciting thing I'd ever done.

Doctor, Astronaut, Firefighter, Entrepreneur

Becoming an entrepreneur is a dream, in the same way people dream about becoming a doctor, astronaut, or firefighter. It should not be a means to an end, but a thirst that needs to be quenched.

After my experience selling seeds I started a new business every summer. Before I could legally work, I'd pretty much sold everything from bracelets to fruits and vegetables, to newspaper subscriptions, to chocolates, to milk … you name it.

From the age of 10, I'd go into my room at the end of every day to count the money I'd made and keep track of it in a ledger using graph paper. I'd write down whether I'd made a profit or loss: The gains would be written in blue, and the losses in red. I did not become an entrepreneur — it was already in me just waiting to get out.

You need to be passionate about it or you may not make it through. I'd say it's comparable to people who dream about becoming professional dancers. They love to dance so much that they fill every waking hour with dancing. People who attend a class only once a week don't stand a chance beside the person who can't stop dancing.

If it's not a passion — if it's not something that you find yourself doing naturally — I'd seriously reconsider becoming an entrepreneur.

My First and Last Job

In December 2005 I graduated from Sheridan College's 3-year marketing diploma program and had little to no idea what my next steps were. I wanted to start a company, but I didn't have a grandiose *aha* moment and I knew that I didn't understand most things about running a small business. (I never advise that anyone start a business right out of school. If you've never worked in your field before, it will take years to learn key lessons that you could have learned in months working for someone else.)

My first job offer came from small-business owner Tim Mischuk at Bluetree Direct Inc., which specialized in building web-to-print SaaS (software as a service) for printers across the United States and Canada. I really had no idea what I was doing for the first few months, but I was eager to learn.

Over the next 2-1/2 years I went from being a completely green project manager to hiring and managing a large development team, flying around the continent conducting software implementations and setting up all of the things needed to run a successful SaaS. It was during this time that I learned the majority of what I would need to operate a small business: how to host an effective conference call, how to manage a statement of work, how to deal with difficult customers, how to on-board a new customer ... the list goes on. You just can't learn these things in school. Besides, it's best to do it while collecting a weekly paycheque and being around people who can help you navigate these lessons.

Looking back, I definitely wasn't qualified for the position when I took it, which admittedly led to some dark days and even a few tears, but I got the work out the door. During one staff meeting a colleague described me as one of the hardest working yet least-paid people in the company, and I took it as a compliment. I pushed hard every single day as if the company were my own, and I owned 100% of every issue my customers had.

I earned my stripes helping that small company grow to the point where it was acquired by a larger firm. During the acquisition of what the larger firm described as a "recession-proof business" we were promised job security *(ROFL)*.

The Layoff

Six months later, the acquiring company gathered most of us into the boardroom and informed us that we were all being laid off because "the great recession" had hurt their quarterly earnings and they needed to cut employees across the board. I was escorted out the door directly after the meeting.

That day I realized that working a corporate job was in fact full of risk. The person who laid me off didn't know what I did, didn't know about my new family, and had no idea that I was working on a ton of very important projects that they didn't have a plan to complete. In a corporation, that's just how it happens. If you think you have job security in a big corporation, you need a reality check.

I had to go home to my pregnant wife and tell her that even though I had been performing very well at work, I was strategically laid off because of poor quarterly earnings. I should have probably been more worried at this point, but I knew that I could either gripe about the past or move forward with my future.

Declare Your Future

When I got home, my incredible wife Tammy asked the question that you have to ask yourself when faced with such an event: "What are you going to do?"

Although I responded quickly, my answer had been percolating in my mind for over a year: I'm going to start a digital marketing company and everything is going to be great.

Not *okay*, it was going to be *great*. If I was going to dedicate my work life to something, it had to be great.

You see, tons of my customers had asked me if I knew anyone in digital marketing. More specifically, they asked me questions like:

How do I get my website to rank at the top of Google?

Why doesn't my website convert people into customers?

How can I generate sales leads through a landing page?

How do I measure success from my online advertising?

Do you know anyone who can help me launch a Google AdWords campaign?

Back then I saw a lot of companies offering digital marketing services, but it didn't seem like anyone had the full picture. No one did it well. No one made it beautiful. No one made it simple.

Now, I'll admit that I didn't have any of the soft skills needed to actually launch such a service. I didn't know how to use Photoshop/InDesign/Illustrator/Dreamweaver, nor did I know how to code in PHP/HTML/CSS, but I knew how to find those people. My lack of skills forced me to rely on others to do the work, meaning that it was never my main vocation to service clients. It was my calling to build this business.

People thought that my decision to start a new company with only 8 weeks of severance to help buy food for my family and keep a roof over our head was a massive risk, but I never saw it that way. I started a company because I wanted to eliminate the risk of getting laid off again. I never wanted to be walked to the door again, and I knew that I was the only person on this planet who wouldn't fire me. Maybe I was wrong, but I didn't see any other option than to start a company. My family needed it. I needed it. Customers needed it.

Everyone should take stock of the risks that surround them in their lives and feel grateful for what they have. Nothing is guaranteed. Corporate jobs are a risk. Starting a company is a risk. Staying in the same job for 30 years is a risk. Not doing anything is a risk.

Make a declaration about your future today. What are you going to do? Say it out loud to yourself — if you don't, life will just pass you by. Tell your significant other, tell your friends, and, most importantly, *tell yourself.* Have conviction in what you're about to do. Talk about how you're going to sell your product, how you're going to expand, and what your 5-year goals are. Something powerful happens when you declare your plans to yourself and others: You'll begin to gain momentum toward reaching your goals.

MAKE A DECLARATION ABOUT YOUR FUTURE TODAY.

Once you start speaking your goals aloud to the people around you, you can't easily take them back. Those people will remind you of your vision when times are tough and keep you accountable to what you've declared. If people around you are supportive, they will constantly remind you of your declaration and help you achieve it. If you stay accountable to your own declarations, each decision that you make will start to align with your declarations and move you closer to your end goal.

IGNORE THE NAYSAYERS. APPROVE YOURSELF. CONVINCE YOURSELF.

When you make declarations about your future, prospective customers will become early adopters to join you in your vision. Vendors will come alongside you to help provide you with their products and services. Other entrepreneurs will encourage you and provide you with advice to navigate good and bad times. Family will celebrate your successes as you reach your goals.

I often get asked "What is the *one thing* I need to do to have a successful business?" The problem with this question is that it assumes you only need to do *one thing*. If it were that simple, everyone would do that one thing and be wildly successful. Successful entrepreneurs make declarations about their future and routinely follow up with thousands of things in order to achieve their goals. They are relentlessly focused on what they've set out to do.

Making declarations about your future will help you to establish a final destination in your business life, which you can then use to measure all of your decisions against each day.

Embrace Unpredictability

When I started my business, most of my family thought I was being irrational, and some of them tried to offer me advice even though they themselves had no experience starting a business. While most people are well meaning, it's important to realize that you are one of the very few people who has this dream, and other folks, including your loved ones, may not see it the same way.

I'm not saying their concerns are wrong — it's hard to imagine living without a weekly paycheque to keep food on the table — but their concerns are really for themselves and they are simply projecting them onto you. Don't spend time trying to convince them of your plans, because at the beginning your business lives mainly in your head and it will be hard for them to understand. Tell them that you are fine, acknowledge their concerns, and then hang up the phone and get to work because worrying won't make you money.

Ignore the naysayers, some of whom will take pleasure in predicting your failure. People who look for permission or approval from others to start a business will never start. This kind of support is a rare find in most circles so you need your approval and motivation to come from within. Approve yourself. Convince yourself. If you can, find people on the same path who understand your goals. Give yourself permission to ignore everyone else. Critics cannot help you. Most people aren't entrepreneurs, so why should you expect most people to understand and approve of what you are doing?

Starting a company — not to mention the financial instability, daily rejection (yes, this is very real), criticism from others, and loneliness — will challenge every fibre of your being. It's similar to skeleton racing in the Olympics: You train for years in order to hurl yourself down a narrow track with minimal safety gear and a limited sightline. The big difference is that the survival odds are better for the people skeleton racing than people who start a company.

Embrace the unpredictability of being a startup from day one. It's going to be one of the hardest things you'll ever do. But if you succeed, it's worth the pain.

Let's get this thing off the ground.

2

FIRST
STEPS

You've decided to start a company. Congratulations! You are now a student of startups. No one roadmap applies to everyone, so you are going to have to do some research.

When you begin a new business, Google is your friend. Need to learn how to register a business? Google it and start reading through the government forms online. Not sure what kind of business (sole proprietor/partnership/corporation) you are forming? Turn to Google again. Multi-tab your way into answers and learn from every failure. No one has all of the answers, and in the beginning you'll probably be doing it all by yourself, but it needs to get done. Type every question that you have into that browser.

One of my favourite sayings of all time is "Action brings clarity." I'm not sure where I heard it, but it's long been my mantra for launching into new things. If you're not sure how to do something, don't just look at it and wonder. Start trying.

Startup Top 10

With every new business I start (I've launched six companies in my adult professional life so far), I become more confident. I'm so familiar with the process that I can now set up a new company in less than 3 hours. To help you get your new business off the ground, I've prepared a quick list — the essential items you'll need to take care of right away — so you can start generating revenue. This is not an exhaustive list by any means, as every business will have different requirements, but it's a start.

1. Choose Your Business Type

There are three main types of businesses — sole proprietor, partnership, and corporation — and you need to determine what type of business you will be operating. This is a major decision, and I recommend you get a bit of advice from either an accountant or lawyer who can explain the implications of this decision (find someone who you trust right away).

Here is a simplified breakdown of business types in Canada (where I live):

Sole proprietor: You are the business. You can hire people and charge taxes, but everything is registered in your name. You are the sole owner, and all of your taxable earnings (or losses) are attributed to you at the end of the year. You are personally liable for everything. A sole proprietorship is a great way to start because it's cheap to create (less than $100) and, compared to a corporation, requires less accounting to maintain it.

Partnership: Two or more people are the business. A partnership functions in essentially the same way as a sole proprietor except the income and losses are shared by two or more people. I'm not a huge fan of partnerships between non-family members because of the likelihood of disagreements and problems down the road, but if your business is truly a partnership (you are starting it with another person), this is what you need.

Corporation: The company becomes a person. A corporation is more expensive and more complicated to set up (starting at about $600 in my experience), but has very unique advantages. The corporation becomes an entity that can make money and distribute profits or losses to shareholders, which could be just you or many people/businesses. A corporation shields your personal finances from the company in the event of lawsuits where people are going after the entity of a corporation and not you personally. I generally tell people to register as a corporation after they hit $500,000 per year in gross revenue or have amassed a significant amount of intellectual property. A corporation will also enable you to do strategic tax planning. To set up a corporation properly, I recommend hiring a lawyer who specializes in corporations, as they can walk you through the process and ensure your files are in order.

2. Choose a Name

You'll need a company name to complete all of your next steps, so this is important. Coming up with a name that will work for you is no small task, but you need to decide on one quickly if you want to get started.

Company names need to meet four basic requirements:

Be clear and honest. If you are selling custom cakes but people think that your company name sounds like a chair manufacturer, you may want to reconsider your choice. Your prospective customers will make a judgment about your company within seconds of seeing or hearing your name, so it is best to make it easy to understand without needing an explanation. If your name is too vague, you'll need to spend marketing dollars educating your customer about what you do. There are always exceptions to this rule, but it's best to stay clear of any name that needs to be explained.

Originally, I started Candybox as an SEO (search engine optimization) company called CandySEO, but quickly realized that having "SEO" in my name would pigeonhole me as only offering one service. I was going to offer marketing services so I went with the name *Candybox Marketing*, which is a lot broader in scope. I'm so glad I did.

Be unique. If you tell someone the name, they should not easily associate it with another business. It should be memorable enough so that someone can recall it a few days after hearing it. I had a number of people tell me that I should name my agency after myself, Keezer Marketing. Besides the fact that I didn't like the sound of it, and it would limit the business to my personal brand, not many people will remember the name Keezer. But I've come across

TELL PEOPLE WHAT YOU DO WITHOUT FORCING YOURSELF INTO A NICHE.

numerous people that remember Candybox years after they first heard it because it's fun and unique. Their memory of our brand name would typically result in repeat business or even a referral!

Be available. Make sure you can buy the domain name. I still firmly believe that in the United States you need a *.com*, and in Canada you need a *.com* or *.ca*. You want to make it as easy as possible for people to find you, not your competitor! I use **bustaname.com** to help me find good domains.

3. Get a Business Address

If you want your business to grow beyond yourself, you'll need to keep all business activities as separate from your residence as possible, even if you don't plan to have an office space soon. I'll talk more about virtual companies later (see page 91), but if you don't have a physical office space, rent a mailbox with a service so you have an official company address (it costs about $20 per month).

4. Get a Business Phone Number

Remember, you don't want the business to revolve around you, so don't make your personal phone number the main line to the business. I use **voicemailtel.com** to register phone numbers and set up virtual lines that will forward to cell phones. You can set this up in a day, and it costs about $50 per month, depending on usage. Even if you are the only one with an extension, you'll thank me for this later when customers start calling you at all hours of the night.

5. Register Your Business Name

You need to register your business name before you can start doing anything official like opening a bank account, applying for a GST/HST account, or hiring an employee. For legal and tax purposes, you want your business to run separate to your own finances. Visit your provincial or state government business services website to find out how to register your business. It only costs around $60 to register a name in most places and, if you prefer, most municipalities have bricks-and-mortar small business centres where someone can walk you through the process. I just Google my way through the forms. As part of the registration process, you'll need to spend about $20 for a name search to make sure your company name is not already taken.

6. Find an Accountant/Bookkeeper

If this is your first business, you may need some coaching on how to properly prepare your files for annual filing. This includes, but is not limited to, how to invoice your customers, what taxes you need to charge your clients, how to pay yourself, collecting receipts and invoices for write-offs, what things you can and cannot write-off, how often you need to submit your taxes to the government … the list goes on. If you mess up any of these things in the beginning, it may be a full year before you find out you've made a mistake and need to go back and fix it. Avoid this nightmare: A good bookkeeper or accountant will instruct you on what you should keep in mind as you operate your business.

7. Get a Business Bank Account and Credit Card

Once you register your company, open a business chequing account as soon as you can so that you can start accepting and making payments. Remember, you want to keep your personal and business expenses separate (for tax reasons), and this is the easiest way to do it. You'll want to make sure that you can cash that first cheque right away, and you'll need a credit card to sign up for most online services.

8. Get a Logo

You'll need a logo to include on all of your marketing materials (which are imperative if you want to start selling anything), including your business card, website, email, etc. Find a company or designer that can help you navigate the waters of creating an identity for your new company. Branding can cost as little as a few hundred dollars if you use a service like **99designs.com** and as much as five figures if you use a design agency (ahem ... such as Candybox). It's important to create something that communicates your brand's identity and looks professional.

9. Create a Website and Business Cards

Having a website gives you credibility — it lets people know that you are a real business — and it's the modern-day equivalent to a business card. (If you can't communicate what your new company offers quickly and easily on a website, you're in trouble.) Shameless plug: Whenever I start a new business, I use one of my own companies, **launch48.ca**, to set up my website in just 2 days so I have an online presence to which I can start directing people. You will also need a business card. I'll repeat: These things can easily be revised later so do them early rather than wait until everything is perfect. You need to get it done.

10. Start Talking with Prospective Clients

Just because you have a good business idea doesn't mean you know everything. You'll have made a lot of assumptions — pricing, offerings, service area, customer demand, competitive advantages — that you have yet to put into practice. Making the wrong assumptions and sticking to them could be costly, so you need to get your ideas out there in front of potential customers. Not your mom or your friends who will love whatever you sell them, but actual customers who will give you real feedback.

Pitch your business every chance you get. Organize coffees, lunches — anything — to get your ideas out there. Don't assume that your ideas are gold right out of the gate. They need to be

MAKING THE WRONG ASSUMPTIONS COULD BE COSTLY.

refined by fire — your customers — into gold, and their feedback usually burns. If your customers won't buy what you are selling, you don't have a business; you have a bad idea. This doesn't mean that you need to change your idea with every piece of feedback, just that you need to weigh your customers' opinions against your assumptions on a regular basis. Over the past decade I've had the privilege of working alongside successful CEOs and am always shocked to see how many pivots they make in business based on the feedback or influence of others. Entrepreneurs aren't know-it-alls. They are visionaries who intentionally listen to the needs of others.

Fail Forward

When I was growing up, our family had a cottage (also known as a "lake house" or "cabin" if you're not from Ontario, Canada) in this little town called Dorset. The town is so small you might miss it if you blinked, but it's a popular tourist destination because of how cute it is. It has a small bridge, an ice-cream shop, and a scenic lookout tower on top of a hill that most people drive up to view.

From our cottage you could just walk to this tower, and getting to the top was a fun adventure for kids. Every year my best friend

Alex and I would find the most difficult path to the top of the hill, completing a vertical climb up the rock face to get to the tower. Okay, not really, but we were 7 years old, so it seemed like it.

One time when we were going up the hill, Alex told me that if I started to slip (which would probably lead to a major injury and maybe even death) to "fall forward instead of falling backward." Confused by this advice, I asked him why. His answer has stuck with me: "If you fall forward onto your chest on this hill, then you may just get a bit hurt. But if you fall backward down the hill, you won't have a chance to catch yourself and you'll roll down."

Seems a bit silly now, but it's not a bad philosophy. If you are going to fall, purposely fall forward to minimize the damage.

If you see an imminent threat in your first week of business, consider failing forward so you don't lose everything. If you are pitching your idea every day and no one wants to buy it, you need to be real with yourself and consider that you may be headed down the wrong path. If you uncover a barrier that you cannot overcome, a consumer objection that you can't resolve, or even legal issues that you aren't big enough to knock down, consider throwing in the towel early and starting again.

Over the past 10+ years of being an entrepreneur, I've failed more than I've succeeded. But none of my failures has taken me out. Just to prove that failure is part of the journey, here are a few examples of companies that I launched and failed at within a few weeks:

Live-Tweet My Event: A service that live-tweets conferences real-time with trained staff who know how to engage an audience and make any event viral.

DealerGeeks: An automotive software platform that integrates inventory feeds with websites and features a slick lead-generation program to generate new customers.

Jetsbook: An online software that books empty private jets for empty-leg flights that would otherwise go without passengers.

I tried out each one of these companies for a few months and then mothballed it because it wasn't gaining traction in the market. Maybe they could have worked out if I just tried harder. Maybe they are all still good ideas, but I didn't execute them well enough. In the end, I wasn't willing to crash hard because of a good idea.

My Sweet Launch Story

In 2015 I was in the middle of growing Candybox Marketing when I realized that I was turning away 70% of the leads we acquired because of low budgets. As a successful agency, our prices started around $20,000 per project, and tons of small businesses just couldn't afford to hire us. These businesses needed a lot of what we offered in our web services (mobile-responsive websites/WordPress/SEO), but didn't have the budget to make it work. Not only did they want these services for just a few thousand dollars but they

YOU CAN LAUNCH ANYTHING IF YOU GIVE IT EVERYTHING YOU GOT.

also wanted them faster than our typical customers!

In order to meet these customers' needs, we knew that we needed to get rid of everything that would hold a project back. We whiteboarded our entire process from beginning to end, and put everything that delayed a project or took a significant amount of resources on the chopping block.

We imagined ourselves on a sinking ship and threw everything overboard that would slow us down. When you purposely pit yourself against imminent doom, even if it's just imaginary, you start thinking differently and re-evaluate everything. The threat of becoming complacent with the status quo is a great motivator for change.

After evaluating our business model, I came up with a concept for a new company that could create websites in 2 days. In order to do this, I had to reinvent the website-building process. We replaced the design-approval process with on-site collaboration. We replaced our content-writing services with a "Get Ready" package that allowed clients to gather their assets themselves. We replaced custom design and development with incredible website templates. We avoided expensive training by offering in-person on-site website building and training at the same time. We avoided time-consuming back-and-forth email communication with clients by sitting people down at the same table together. By hosting all of the sites and implementing a simple system for going live, we avoided the pains of launching websites with a third-party provider. We stripped everything down and repackaged it as a new product called Launch48.

Launch48 went from original concept to physical opening in 15 business days, including finding an office space and completing renovations, ordering furniture, branding, hiring staff, and finding customers. We were still assembling chairs just hours before we opened our doors to our first customer!

Why did we move so quickly? Before I launch any new idea, I like to verbalize it to potential customers as if it's already a real thing. I believe the only time people give honest feedback is when you provide them with an opportunity to buy and see your product or service. When I first thought of the Launch48 concept, I pitched it to an existing customer — they signed up on the spot! We booked them to come in for their appointment in 3 weeks' time. They had no idea that we didn't even have a space to open our operations. We didn't have an option but to open. People said it couldn't be done, but we opened successfully and launched our first 2-day website with minutes to spare. That was 3 years ago. Launch48 has been packed with customers ever since.

Screw the critic.

Don't Honeymoon

Entrepreneurship has recently become a popular career choice. People love the idea of running their own company. But some people get starry-eyed at the idea of working for themselves and lose sight of what they should be doing. I see it all the time: people who honeymoon in their first month of business. They wake up late since they don't need to be anywhere, and they do whatever they want during the day. They meet with whomever they want to, even friends and family during business hours. Some people even start running errands when they should be closing deals. This is a good sign they have no idea what it takes to start a business.

The freedom to travel, set your own schedule, and sleep in late may come after years of building a good company, but the first few weeks are not the appropriate time. That's when you need to push hard, work late, and make it rain. In a few weeks or months you may be out of money. Even if you get clients, cash flow is an unforgiving beast for most new startups. It's a race against the clock.

Your first few weeks should be packed. You'll be exhausted from the details you need to organize, decisions you need to make, and all the running around you need to do to get your business off the ground. If you've moved over from the corporate world, you may be enjoying your new-found freedom where someone isn't watching your every move, but now you are the one who needs to push yourself forward.

Like any rocket launch, when the first few seconds require a lot of energy just to move a few feet, you'll only gain momentum by pushing in the moment. It will be hard, it will be unforgiving, but if it works, it will be worth the pain.

STARTUP
CASH

Our generation has been tarnished by TV shows that glorify startups pitching investment groups. You know what I'm talking about: Someone walks on stage and pitches their idea to a panel of investors who either give the money or tear them apart.

I'm not a fan of VCs (venture capitalists) or AIs (angel investors) for every business. Only some businesses need investment, and it often gives a false sense of security to those who obtain it or a false sense of failure to those who don't.

Investment companies are not looking for you to succeed personally. Let's be honest: They want to get a return. Once you start winning, you need to start paying these people back (with a lot of interest) or constantly feed them a share of your profits. You're basically married to someone who you may not know very well, and they are in it for themselves.

I understand that some kinds of businesses cannot start without capital. Some businesses need stock, capital equipment, a warehouse, tons of staff, or a financial runway so that the product can be finished. But these days many businesses can get off the ground with under $5,000.

The cost of setting up a business has plummeted over the last 30 years. In a lot of industries, the barriers to entry have been lowered, allowing new entrants access to the latest technology for a small monthly fee or for free.

In early 2000, you would have needed tens of thousands of dollars just to equip an office, including phones, email, server, etc. You don't need that anymore. You can acquire these items on your first day before lunch — if you know what you're doing. I'll talk more about this in Chapter 9: Automation Hacks, which outlines tons of software you can employ to eliminate major costs in a typical business.

The bottom line is that if you are waiting for finances to get started, you may never take that first step. If you need money, scrape and save as much as you can. You may have the next big business idea that no one wants to invest in. You may see an opportunity that no one else does. You may be ready to own your own future.

You *need* to have skin in the game. Don't let others determine your future because your business doesn't meet their investment portfolio.

Find Startup Customers

Instead of finding startup investors, find startup customers. These are the people who are willing to buy your product before it has launched, or maybe buy it when it's still under development with a final delivery date in mind. These people are willing to risk spending their money on you while you are just getting off the ground. In my very first week of busi-

YOU NEED TO HAVE SKIN IN THE GAME.

ness, I generated around $10,000 from companies that ordered our services before we had any resemblance of a fully operating company.

You can find startup customers many ways, from crowdsourcing platforms to calling up potential customers. With the growth and popularity of startup companies, consumers have become much more open to investing their dollars before production even begins. People are buying music before it's recorded, new gadgets before they're manufactured, and new cars before the assembly lines are even built.

In 2016, Tesla birthed one of the greatest consumer stories with a single live-streamed event announcing their new $35,000 car. In just one week, Tesla secured over 325,000 preorders for their new electric car, generating an estimated $14 billion of future sales for the company. Looking at these consumer numbers, I call this the greatest consumer product launch in the history of mankind.

Tesla didn't sell 325,000 cars in one week, as the cars didn't even exist. They had not even broken ground on their production facility at the time of the live-stream. They sold $1,000 deposits for the idea of 325,000 cars. The preorders came from people who had never seen the car in person, never taken it for a test drive or felt what it was like to sit in it. They didn't know how it handled, didn't know what it smelled like, and weren't sure if their kids would like the back seat. Tesla proved their business case with a single model car, a live-stream, and a single-page website that took deposits online.

When I was laid off, I could have spent a lot of time filling out forms for grants, loans, or investors. Instead I spent all of my time finding my startup customers. It's hard to do both, and I chose to go the customer route.

Having startup customers is amazing because it does a lot more than just give you a bank balance. These customers help inform your product/service right from day one. Instead of working in a vacuum surrounded by finance people, you get live feedback from real people who actually want to use your company.

Tesla didn't need to impress a lot of investors with car specs. They shocked them with preorders and their stock responded in kind.

Startup customers also prove your business is needed, that what you have is needed in the marketplace. You can have all of the investors in the world, but if people don't want to buy your goods, you have a lot of debt and no business. If you can find one customer who wants to buy what you are selling, there are probably hundreds or thousands of customers out there waiting for your product.

On the other hand, if you can't find a single person to say yes, your idea may not be that good to begin with. Looking for startup customers is a great way to stop a bad idea before it gets too far.

Over the past decade, I've had the privilege of working alongside over 100 CEOs and founders from a variety of industries. What do they have in common? They all are willing to pivot their business ideas, products, and models based on qualified consumer feedback. People may perceive CEOs to be persistent and unwavering in their efforts, but I believe the opposite is true: Great CEOs are in tune with customer feedback and are willing to do what it takes to make them happy. People who we consider to be visionaries aren't just looking into the future, but are looking to solve the problems of today for your average customer.

I understand that finding startup customers may not work for all business models, but consider it before you start racking up debt (and risk).

Determine Your MVP

If you haven't heard this term yet, you need to look it up. "Minimal viable product" (MVP) is essentially the least investment you need to make a passable product in your marketplace. Don't wait until you have a perfect product to get it in front of your market; build it in phases. See what it would take to get a great Version 1 out, and then gather feedback.

When you speak with CEOs on a regular basis, you'll hear stories of their first year in business and how immature their product/service was, but they got it to market anyway. You can change your product/service over time — improve it, enhance it — but you need

GET IT OUT THE DOOR AND IN FRONT OF YOUR CUSTOMERS.

to start getting your product out as soon as you can to prove your model.

When I started Candybox, I had no choice but to outsource development to a third party in order to turn a profit. It was not perfect, but it worked. It gave me the capital I needed to continue to move my business forward, and eventually I had enough work to hire full-time staff to produce excellent work. Everyone always has a first generation of their service. You need to start somewhere.

Launch early, launch often, launch daily. Get it out the door and in front of your customers.

Don't Work for Free

Don't fall into this trap. I'm not talking about unpaid internships that can give you an education in an industry. We millennials live in a time of unpaid internships, where we need to invest our time to get our foot in the door. There aren't enough jobs to go around, and very few companies are willing to pay for training like they did for previous generations. I've worked these jobs, paid my dues, and would do it again in a heartbeat. It got me into the industry that I wanted to specialize in.

I'm talking about launching a new business and offering to work for free just to get a few customers. Don't do it. Working in a job for free is different than working for free while you're trying to build a company.

In my early days, I'd hear the following at least once a week:

"Once you launch my website, you can list your name on the bottom and you'll get tons of traffic!"

"I'll refer all of my friends to you. I'm very connected."

"I can be a reference for you going forward."

Barf. Avoid these cheapskates. If your service is valuable, they should compensate you for your time and efforts. Remember: A company is not just about your time. You have staff or contractors to pay, and everyone needs to eat.

I'm not against discounting. If any prospect dangles the future opportunity of referrals over your deal, try putting the ball back in their court and see what happens: "Sure, I'd love the referral! How about this: After you give me five paying customers, I'll do your project at my cost." My guess is that you'll immediately see these people shrink back, realizing they never really had the ability to produce what they promised. Leave these conversations.

I never worked for free during my startup phase, and I'm very happy I made this decision on day one. It would have stagnated my growth, cheapened my service, or, even worse, attracted more terrible nonpaying clients. Time is worth money. The time that you might spend on free or almost-free work is time that you are not spending finding real clients. I cannot stress this enough: You are losing every minute you spend working for free.

Once you are out of the startup phase, you may decide to give away work for free as you'll have a sustainable business that can afford the time and resources. But during startup, you have a very short runway to get the plane off the ground. Your runway (cash) will run out faster than you think, and failing to lift off may have some catastrophic consequences.

BE THE
BUSINESS
PLAN

Business plans are like underwear: They need to be changed every day.

Whoa, whoa, whoa, Darrell, but what about the 5-year financial plan? Isn't that what they've taught in business schools since the dawn of time? Short answer: kind of.

Five-year business plans are great for understanding all of the key factors (internal and external) that a business needs to consider before starting. They force you to look at aspects of the business that you may not have considered and are an incredible way to point out blind spots in your overall plan. Do a quick Google search on "5-year business plan" and you'll find a plethora of spreadsheets, pitch decks, and Word documents that can help you build a plan that you could present to a bank or financial investor, but don't put all of your trust in this one-time exercise.

A typical person who is looking to start a business can complete the first few pages of a business plan, including the problem they are trying to solve and their proposed solution. A lot of people stop there and believe that by simply identifying the solution, they have a business. This is where we separate entrepreneurs from *wantrepreneurs.* Entrepreneurs will work beyond this to figure out the rest of their business plan, whereas wantrepreneurs think that simply because they can solve the problem they are entitled to make the big bucks.

The rest of the business plan would include things like market research, competitor analysis, financial model for profit, validation of your solution actually solving the problem, market segmentation, identification of your target market and buying habits, market trends (including growth or decline), future markets, competitive advantages, marketing and sales plan, facilities, technology, equipment, key performance indicators, milestones, organizational structure, management methodology, revenue/sales forecasts, expenses/budget, projected profit/loss, cash flow, and a nice summary pulling it all together. Exhausted yet? It *should* exhaust you, because most people are good at a few of these areas but not all of them.

If you major in sales and marketing, you may have an incredible strategy to sell your product/service, but if you can't deliver, you have an operational nightmare on your hands. Customers will never buy again if you can't deliver the first time. You need to consider *everything* when you are starting a business, and not be overwhelmed by it all at once.

You Are the Business Plan

When you first start off, you should create a traditional business plan as a good discipline, but you need to become the business plan. You should be able to easily articulate any area of the business (marketing/sales/operations/finance) to anyone who asks. And you need to use everything that you absorb in the outside world to continually measure against your plan, change your plan, or encourage your plan.

Although I am a strong believer in downtime, which I discuss later (see page 58), you need to come to terms with the fact that your business will consume most of your spare thinking time. You'll fall asleep thinking about your next campaign and wake up thinking about the things you need to accomplish.

It frightens me when people want to start a business but not devote the majority of their waking time to it (at least in the beginning). The dream of starting a business and having nothing to do with it is a very strange dream. Making lots of money by doing as little work as possible is some kind of fairy tale told at multi-level marketing pep rallies but does not apply in the real world. If you don't want to put your own skin in the game, you have no chance at winning. If it is truly that easy to make money,

CUSTOMERS WILL NEVER BUY AGAIN IF YOU CAN'T DELIVER THE FIRST TIME.

you either have some kind of strange monopoly or have inherited someone else's hard work for which they've paid the price. If it truly doesn't take any work, look out, because your competition will be coming in very soon to take you down. That's how a free market works.

Prizes come at the end of the race, not the beginning. If you want to win the race, you have to practice every day. Wake up early, push hard, tear metaphoric muscles, exceed your limits, throw up in a garbage can, wipe away the remnants from your lip, and keep going.

Eat, drink, and sleep the plan. *Be the plan.*

Revise the Plan in the Shower

When I first started Candybox I would think about my business plan every single morning while taking a shower. The shower was my time. My time to think about the big picture without the distractions of the day begging for my attention.

Each morning as scalding-hot water hit my back I'd visualize my day, my week, my month. I'd calculate cash flow, review opportunities, think about threats, make plans, adjust plans, change everything. Every day I spend time in the morning in quiet meditation, getting rid of yesterday's failures so I can plan for today's successes.

Giving yourself time to reflect each day helps you take control of your day before it happens to you. People don't grow companies by accident; they do it by making plans and executing them every single day. Some of your best ideas and decisions will come at times when you aren't responding to the needs of others, but reflecting on the needs of the company as a whole.

One of the greatest pitfalls of entrepreneurs is to work too much *in* the business and neglect working *on* the business. It's easier said than done, which is why you need to approach every single day with a clear head and action plan for growing the business. If you aren't proactive in growth, you'll easily find yourself busy in the day-to-day needs of your business.

Don't put your stake in the ground and walk away. Treat your business plan as a living document and give yourself time to review and revise it on a regular basis.

Change or Die

It's a popular motto for a reason.

It's incredible to see the amount of change that has occurred in every industry over the last 200 years, and it keeps speeding up. Fifty-year-old companies are a thing of the past. Now, few companies make it at all and even the largest will fall if they aren't careful.

Your customer's habits, needs, requirements, and demographics change every single year. If you're not watching these changes and matching them, you will be obsolete before you can deliver on that fantastic 5-year business plan that you have in your office drawer. You need to change every year.

CEOs and business leaders are often portrayed as unshakeable, unmoving, unchangeable. This isn't accurate. People confuse a stubbornness to succeed with a stubborn refusal to change. If a CEO wants to be successful, they will change all of the time. They are in business because they become experts at what their customers want, or will want one day, not because customers listen to and follow what they say. Great leaders don't stick to their guns, they become experts

IF YOU NEGLECT TO CHANGE, YOUR COMPANY WON'T MAKE IT.

at knowing what they need to change to continue being relevant.

You can tell a company is about to go under when it keeps doing the same thing over and over again expecting to continue growing. Recently, Sears went under in Canada because it had become redundant. There was no good reason to go to Sears. They didn't change. Their customers started retiring and moving on. Their online store sucked. They could have revived themselves, but it would have taken a major overhaul, and when they did start trying, it was too little too late.

Every stage of your company growth will require you to change what you do and how you do it. Teams of 3 operate differently than teams of 30 and teams of 300. It's stupid to think that your business can double in size and everything can operate in the same way. I'm constantly reading books like *Scaling Up* by Verne Harnish or *Good to Great* by Jim Collins as I learn how to change my everyday job in order to nurture company growth.

When you are a sole proprietor (see page 14), it's easy to stay organized because you can pretty much keep track of everything in your head. You have a fairly good idea about deals in the pipeline, cash flow, product development, operational issues, and every little detail about your customer. But as soon as you add your first employee, your job changes. You need to communicate and be communicated with. Multiply that a few times and you should have a giant web of communication between departments to ensure that you can still execute flawlessly as a large company.

Every year you should evaluate your own schedule to find out what you can change to better serve the future of the company. Here are some basic questions to ask yourself:

What am I spending my time on during the average week? (break it down by tasks and percentages)

How many of these tasks can be delegated to another team member, or become a new position in the company?

Where is my time best spent in the company to help it grow?

In what area do I need to allocate more time to growth?

How can I best communicate these changes to my team?

If you neglect to change your company, your job, and your plans to match your growth, your company won't make it.

PICK UP
YOUR
FREAKIN'
PHONE

If you want to run a business, you need to use your phone.

I started out writing this chapter specifically for millennials (born 1980 to 1995) and even up-and-coming Gen Zs (born 1995+), but I think we can all agree that since the introduction of the smartphone most people have gotten out of the habit of actually talking on the phone. This is tragic. Pardon me if this doesn't apply to you, but it has to be said.

Your phone itself is the most important tool on your smartphone, above social media, email, or online banking. Knowing how to use it can mean the difference between a business that is surviving and one that is thriving. If I had to keep just one app — you've guessed it — it would be the phone.

I picked up my phone on my first day in business as Candybox Marketing and didn't give in. I was ruthless. I called everyone I knew to talk to them about digital marketing. Sure, it would have been easier to send an email to all of my contacts, but emails don't put a demand on people to give you an answer. Only you can do that.

Push Sales

From the ages of 12 to 16 I went door to door selling subscriptions to newspapers to make money. I was on 100% commission. If I got four customers in an evening, I'd be treated out to fast food. It was an incredible motivator. I learned the patience and persistence needed to get sales.

When selling subscriptions like that, an average salesperson might only get 1 order for every 100 doors knocked on. For years I worked at it every week in extreme cold, snow, wind, rain — it didn't matter. If the weather was terrible, it became part of my strategy: Make people feel so bad that I was out in the cold that they'd invite me into their homes; as a result, I'd have a better chance of winning them as a customer. It took persistence.

Millennials get a bad rap for being lazy. I don't know where this came from, but from what I've read, the same rhetoric has been applied to just about every young generation. The baby boomers were lazy when they were young, Gen-Xers were lazy, and now it's our turn. It's hard to believe that millennials are lazy when you look at the stats, though: Millennials are one of the most-educated generations in all history, with the most post-secondary education. Lazy people don't go to university for 5 years.

However, I have found that millennials occasionally lack the habits that make someone successful, and one of those habits is using an actual phone. We (I'm including myself here as a millennial) hate phone calls, but some of us are just one call away from landing that next job or next big customer. We need to adapt to a world that may work in ways that make us feel uncomfortable. Millennial or not, if this is your biggest barrier between success and failure, isn't it worth learning a new skill?

But Darrell, you say, *aren't you in the business of lead-generation through digital marketing?* I certainly am. Every day I generate leads from people searching online, but I typically follow up with them by phone. Some of my largest customers initially contacted me via a phone call as well, people who decided to skip our online lead-generation strategy and get someone on the phone right away. Sometimes our sales aren't growing like they should and I need to get new customers in the door. I can't sit around waiting for them to come in. I'm a business owner; it's my responsibility to go get them.

YOU NEED TO GET ON YOUR FREAKIN' PHONE.

When you start up, you need to get on your freakin' phone. Call every connection you have and let them know what you are doing. Ask them if you can help them. Ask them for the business. If nothing else, ask them if they know anyone who could use your product/service and how you can contact them. Identify a problem you could help them solve. Get something from the call. Give something during the call. Make it worth their time and yours.

Understand the Basics

This may sound absurd, but many people don't know how to talk on the phone (I learned how to use the phone effectively early on because I had to). I'll call someone and they'll answer without saying which company they work for or their name. For example:

(Me calling to interview someone.)

Ring, ring

Them: Hello?

Me: Uh, hello? Who is this?

Them: Uh … it's David.

Me: Hey, David. It's Darrell. I'm calling about the interview? Is it still a good time to talk?

Them: Yeah.

(I proceed to interview them knowing that they don't have any phone skills.)

I know it may sound lame and old fashioned, but if you want to communicate with customers, you'll need to learn some phone skills.

Here are a few basic pointers:

- Answer your phone with a proper greeting announcing your name and company name. Most people find this

awkward and lame at first, but it helps the caller understand who they are speaking with.

- Sound positive when you answer the phone.
- Understand the dynamics of how to lead a phone discussion.
- Know how to generate a friendly demeanor and engage in small talk when appropriate.
- Leave a proper voicemail message with clear instructions on how the other party should follow up.
- Have an agenda for every call you make and make it clear to the other party why you are calling.
- Respond to voicemail messages within the same business day on which they were received.
- Email a summary of what was discussed/agreed upon in the call.
- If you are cold-calling, work with the receptionist to get the right person on a call.
- Learn how to set up and lead a teleconference and/or web meeting with your own agenda.

Don't Let Opportunity Go to Voicemail

I can't tell you how many big opportunities have been presented to me just by answering the phone: Prospects needing work done who are then converted to customers. Competitors wanting to collabo-rate. People calling for help or advice. Opportunity calls every day.

I know picking up the phone puts a demand on our time and so our first inclination is to avoid it. Our heart rate increases when an unknown number displays on our screen and we ask ourselves:

Who is it?

What if they want to sell me something?

Is this going to waste my time?

Is it an overseas telemarketing company trying to clean my windows? How do I get rid of them?

It really doesn't take a lot to mentally reframe these questions and turn that ringing phone into a positive experience:

Is this my next big opportunity?

Does someone need my help?

I wonder if they are calling because they found my website online and want to order?

Is this an existing customer that needs help? If I answer, could I keep their business?

Guess what? You have 15 seconds to decide before that person goes to voicemail and may disappear forever. Sometimes callers don't leave voicemail. Some customers will immediately call someone else and sign up on the spot, becoming someone else's customer, and your chance is gone *forever*. This fact should scare you.

All of that time and effort you spent getting your name out there is for naught because you didn't want to answer your phone. I'm not being dramatic; it's real life. Recently we were filming some customer testimonials for our work, and a CEO said he went with us because he called a number of firms and I was the only one who picked up my phone. It's not that I sit around doing nothing, I just know the value of picking up the phone *every single time.*

Common Objections to Answering the Phone

Okay, let me refute some of your objections to picking up that ringing phone right now:

What if it's a telemarketer?

Well, so what if it is? If it's a telemarketer, politely ask them to take you off their list and hang up. Talk over them. Make it snappy — 10 seconds of your time and you're done. At least you know who it was and you're now off their call list.

What if I'm somewhere noisy?

I choose to pick up the phone no matter where I am. People understand that in this day and age you aren't chained to a desk somewhere and that you are a real person. Real people get out of the office. Real people get coffee. So what? Answer your phone and if you can't hear very well, you can at least commit to calling them back when you are in a better position. They'll appreciate getting a quick answer more than needing to leave a long voicemail message.

What if I'm in a meeting?

This depends on who you're meeting with. If you're with a client, it would be incredibly rude to accept a call when a current customer needs your attention. But if you are meeting with a friend who won't mind a quick intermission, or if you are attending an internal meeting and you aren't a major contributor, excusing yourself from the room for a few minutes could generate that next opportunity.

What if I'm driving?

I currently drive a very loud car. It's got a 5.0L V8 engine (which is stupid big if you don't know anything about cars) and it doesn't mask the sound very well. But it automatically connects to my phone, so when I'm in my car I can make and receive calls. When someone calls me, I just answer it, even though I know they can hear my obnoxious car. What do I have to lose? As long as I'm hands-free, I'm not breaking any laws or doing anything else with my time.

If it's a big prospect calling, they now know three things about me: I pick up my phone and am available to them; I'm a busy guy on the run; and I have an interesting car (hopefully they are into that). Those aren't bad things. I have closed tons of deals while driving and you can, too. Answer your freakin' phone.

Phone Success Stories

Before you let that next call go to voicemail, consider some of these major successes I've enjoyed simply because I answer my phone on a regular basis.

- I'm driving back from a customer's location in Barrie, Ontario. I listen to a voicemail that was left during my meeting and then quickly call them back. It's a large association that wants to attend our social media workshop. I pull over to the side of the road and provide them with the details and discuss the program. They go on to buy $150,000 of services from us and send us at least 4 new customers per year of equal size.

- A lady who wants to know more about our workshop calls me. I spend 30 minutes on the call with her answering questions about every segment of our program. She ends up buying a ticket for $299 and attends the event. Big win, eh? Two years later she buys a business and refers me to the other partner, which turns out to be over $100,000 in annual revenue over the past 6 years. Major win.

- A student calls saying he would like to interview me. I end up meeting up with him later that day for a coffee and hire him as a co-op student for the summer. Today that same guy is running more than half of Candybox and has launched some of our biggest projects.

- I'm walking into my studio when I get a call from a famous keynote speaker. He just saw my videos online, found my number, and called me out of the blue with no agenda. We hit it off. We grab a coffee to discuss keynote speaking. I was just getting into that game, speaking at about 50 events per year. Since then we've been trading customers and swapping notes about what's working in the industry, and we even have a beer once in a while. Awesome sauce.

- I'm working from home, my kids are shouting in the background, and I pick up the phone anyway. A guy wants to grab a coffee to sell me on his services. He thinks that we could benefit one another with referrals. I meet up with him, and since then we've traded at least $300,000 of business with one another. We partner with his firm to get into a new industry and help him grow along the way. *Boom shakalaka.*

Yes, I also get one or two telemarketing calls a day. They are an annoying fact of life, but I don't let that stop me from answering my next opportunity.

Make the Call

No one wants to be a telemarketer, but do you know what's worse? Going out of business. Sometimes you just need to call a prospect to become a new customer. You need to make the call to follow up on the contract, proposal, or deal that they asked for. You need to make the call to touch base with your best client and see how they are doing.

THERE'S NO WAY TO AUTOMATE YOUR RELATION-SHIPS.

Make the call. Pick up the phone. There's no way to automate your relationships on this level.

As per HubSpots' *State of Inbound Marketing 2018 Report,* phone calls combined with email are still the top method used by salespeople to generate new customers. Phone calls are hard to make, and you'll hear a lot of voicemail messages, but you need to push through the rejection. If you only get 1 customer for every 50 calls that you make, you now have a number that you can use to motivate yourself every day: "If I make 100 calls per day, I'll generate 2 customers per day and 10 per week." You need real grit to work the phone all day, but it's work that needs to get done. Once you start generating sales, you'll be motivated to hit the phones even harder than you did before.

Pick up your freakin' phone and enjoy the results.

6

BUILD THE BEST JOB EVER

What good is building a company that you hate working for? Many people don't consider their end game when they are just getting started. I speak in front of a lot of CEO/executive groups and frequently hear their complaints and horror stories (past and current) of how much of a pain their company is.

Think about it: You started the company. You architected the company. You laid the foundation of the company *but you hate your job.* It sounds stupid, but it happens all the time.

Just because you *can* build a company doesn't mean that it's the right company for you. Just because something is profitable doesn't mean that you should do it. If you are starting out, you are in control of your destiny.

One of my all-time favourite quotations is "I am the master of my fate: I am the captain of my soul" from a poem by William Ernest Henley (1849–1903). It rings even truer if you are a business owner.

You are the one who has the power to change anything you want, for good or bad.

Know What You Value

When you start your company, you need to ensure that you aren't just building a terrible job that you need to fill but an amazing company that you love to run. After all, you alone are the captain.

Start by understanding your values. What things do you value more than anything else in the world?

Are you a family person? Build that into the plan.

Do you value making obscene amounts of money? Make sure your plan is obscenely profitable.

Do you want to enjoy lots of time off? Build a company that can operate without you.

Do you love having evenings and weekends free? Choose a 9-to-5 business.

Do you just want to pursue a specific passion that may not be profitable? Count the cost of other opportunities.

Very few people share the exact same values, which means that each person should have a different plan.

I loved reading the biography of Steve Jobs, and while his story inspires me, I also disagree with a number of his life decisions. He worked long hours and it appears to have taken a toll on his personal life. I'm not willing to sacrifice my family for profits. Never. So I've built my business in such a way that it doesn't take over my life.

BUILD A JOB THAT YOU'LL LOVE IN YEARS TO COME.

As you start your business, make sure that you build it in such a way that you'll still love your job in 10 years' time. I've made a ton of mistakes as I've built my companies, but I've also made adjustments each year to ensure that I still enjoy what I'm doing. For example, I realized that I was passionate about public speaking, so I now dedicate about 30% of my efforts to building this side of the business. I also love taking time off in the summer, so I've built a company where I can work remotely for the majority of July and August. Even though it took over 5 years to reach this goal, it was always in sight and every decision I made led me closer to it.

You have the power to steer your ship in the right direction now so that you don't have to make major adjustments later. Build a job that you'll love in years to come.

Build Your Own Job

I've built my companies so that they align with my values. I know my values may be different than yours, but I want to share some personal examples that you might be able to apply when building your own job.

Value 1: Put family first

One of my biggest values is "family first." People who work for me know this because I tell them as part of their orientation when they join my company. But it's not just my family; I want them to consider theirs as well. In the process of building myself a job that honours family, I've been able to extend this to people who work with me and share the same value.

Value 2: Work only 9 to 5

In an industry that typically works 8 a.m. to 6:30 p.m., I work 9 a.m. to 5 p.m. How? I establish boundaries and work as hard as I can to make every hour count. I believe that if you set up these boundaries from the beginning, people will work hard enough to ensure that their work is done on time and they won't be prone to wasting it. Quality of workmanship over quantity of hours wins every time. Every day I prioritize my tasks and get as many done as I can in a day.

This also means that I have to communicate clearly to my customers that I don't work after 5 p.m. If you start answering texts or emails at 6 p.m. or 9 p.m., you're actually training your customers to expect that you are always available. My customers rarely call me during the evening or on the weekend — they know I won't answer. I've set a healthy boundary to ensure my values are left intact. At 5 p.m., I close my laptop and am no longer Darrell Keezer, CEO of

Candybox. I'm Daddy. If my customers don't like that, they can choose another firm.

SET SOME GOALS TO MAKE AN IMPACT.

I was speaking to a competitor recently, and he was complaining that one of their customers keeps messaging them on Facebook Messenger at all hours of the night. I was with him when he answered this client on his phone, all the while complaining about how terrible it was. I gently told him that it was actually his fault. He allowed them to connect with him on Facebook. He answered their questions outside of work hours. He immediately responded to every request. He trained his client to abuse his time, and they were a willing participant. Set your boundaries or your customers will walk all over you.

Value 3: Life is about more than money

My work should have a positive impact on the world. Call it lame, but I don't want to work for money; I want money to work for me. Every year I prioritize things like volunteering at the local food shelter with my team, donating to charities that are making a difference, and offering a substantial discount to certain charities in order to help them with their digital marketing. I don't do it to get recognition; it just feels good to help. I want to look back at our work and feel a sense of pride, so I make it a priority. Find your purpose in this world and set some goals to make an impact, even if they are small to begin with.

Value 4: Work alongside awesomeness

I'm very involved during the hiring process for each of my companies because I love to work in a positive environment. I'm not saying that everyone needs to be happy-go-lucky and never stop smiling, but they can't have toxic attitudes. I work hard during the interview process to weed out anyone who might bring negativity to the organization and to focus on finding people who are really passionate about our mission. Choose people who you'd go camping with over people who only have the skills that you need. Skills can be taught but attitudes generally don't change.

Value 5: Take ownership and know when to delegate

When you start your company, you may need to do everything yourself. You're the owner, so it's up to you to own whatever no one else does. Over time, however, you need to delegate the tasks that you can't do/don't like doing/aren't good at. As you grow, it becomes critical to hire people who can handle different tasks properly and take ownership for you. Over time I realized that I loved working on the sales end of the business, speaking in front of groups, and leading the team. I gradually started to delegate tasks that I didn't have time for in order to focus on tasks that I loved doing. I now spend most of my time meeting with prospective customers, speaking at events, and encouraging the team. It's good to do a quarterly review of your entire task list to see what you can delegate to others or if you need to hire someone to take the load. Sounds simple enough, but a ton of CEOs hold on to these tasks because of bad habits and a sense of duty. Let them go and watch your business grow!

Value 6: Eliminate things I hate

Why build a business that contains things that you hate? Here's a quick list of things that I've eliminated because I had the power to do so:

- **Clutter:** I have a strict clean-desk policy and enforce it. (Maybe a little too much. Sorry, guys.)
- **Paper:** We don't have a printer in our studio. You heard me. No printer = no paper.
- **Long meetings:** Most of the meetings I plan are 15 minutes long, no longer. If you want to have a 1-hour meeting, you better have a really good reason because I hate wasting time (see Value 1).
- **Being tied to a desk:** I've set up everything in my company to work virtually so that I can work from anywhere, anytime.

Those are just a few examples, but it's important to recognize that as a leader, you have the choice to set up a company that you love.

Find Awesome Customers

This may offend some people (sorry!), but there are some customers I love working with, and some I don't. Different industries attract

STOP WORKING WITH CUSTOMERS YOU HATE.

different kinds of people, and sometimes working with these customers takes everything out of you. I've learned this lesson time and time again when I've accepted a customer I'm unsure about only to find out a year later that we were better off never to have had their business.

Determine which customers you love working with and give them your all. You'll be passionate about their projects, and they'll feel it. They will appreciate your amazing work, and you'll naturally get referrals and new business every single day. It's amazing what can happen when you love your customers and they love you right back.

We probably all have different definitions of what makes a terrible customer. It could be people who don't pay their bills on time. It could be people who treat you poorly. It could be people who give you menial or boring work you have no interest in. In the process of finding your ideal customer, you need to define who is not ideal for you.

A friend of mine owns a successful business but works in a sector with terrible customers. Let me tell you, he is miserable on a regular basis. He acts as though he has no choice, but he does. He continues to accept the work from bad customers, and the results end up the same every time.

Stop working with customers you hate. I've been known to turn down customers from certain sectors, and I'm proud of it. They are better off without me, and vice versa. For example, recently I was on a sales call and the potential customer was requesting a proposal but was being very vague when describing their business. They wanted us to build a subscription website where people would pay a monthly fee to receive a "mystery package" every month. I asked repeatedly what kind of products customers would be receiving. The conversation went a little like this:

Me: So, what types of products would customer be receiving on a monthly basis?

Prospect: It could be anything. It changes every month.

Me: Could you give me an example of products that one would receive?

Prospect: It could be anything, like a magazine, or maybe a scented candle, or a game.

Me (catching on)**:** Or a sex toy?

Prospect: Yes, we could ship sex toys.

Me: Got it. Well, I can see that you've got a specific market niche that you are pursuing, and I don't think that we'd be a good agency for you. We really love getting excited about the projects that we get to bring to market, and I don't think that my team would be ideal for marketing a monthly sex-toy business.

After which the customer argued for a good 10 minutes that I was being prudish and arrogant to reject her business. I was able to recommend a few other vendors that might be interested in helping her venture, but told her that it wasn't a good fit for our company.

In the end, I know if I want to keep my staff engaged in our work, I need to make sure that I give them work that they'd be proud of. I knew that no one on my team would be excited about selling sex toys and would subsequently start hating their job.

Here are a few questions to ask yourself when pursuing new customers:

Will this relationship be win/win? Will we both walk away happy?

Is this customer a good match for our company culture and values?

Does this customer have a good track record with other vendors?

Am I interested in working with this customer, or do they just represent revenue?

Would I be proud of my work?

Determining if a customer is a good fit doesn't always focus on the end product. You need to consider your company culture. Years ago, I was on a call and a prospect made an offensive remark against millennials in the workforce. I lead a company full of millennials and had to spend the next 15 minutes telling them that we weren't the right company for them. That customer met all of the above requirements positively except I knew they wouldn't work well within our company culture. They left the call upset and didn't understand my reasoning, but I know that they would have been a nightmare for my staff because of their prejudices. A bad customer is not worth losing staff over. Be polite about it, but let them go.

FOCUS ON THE RIGHT METRICS

As an entrepreneur, you need to understand that ideas are cheap. So what if you have great plans? Measure them and set goals. If you aren't making sales, who cares how great your product or service is?

Let me illustrate my point: Every summer I make hamburgers from scratch at least once a week. I get the best ground beef and follow my own recipe. It takes about 40 minutes to prepare these beautiful patties. It also takes great care to cook them on my barbecue. No one is allowed to touch them until they are done. These hamburgers melt in your mouth, and all of my friends love them (or they are just being very polite).

Now consider fast food hamburgers: They are tiny, tasteless, and cooked from frozen. They don't hold a candle to my burgers, and no one in their right mind would ever say they prefer fast food burgers.

Bottom line: I have a better product.

But fast food joints sell billions of burgers every year, and I don't sell any. Why? They have built a business around their product, from location to marketing and pricing and operations. I just have a great idea that no one buys — my family and friends eat them for free.

I have a superior product but lose in every respect when it comes to business sales.

Nobody cares about your service or product if you can't run a business that delivers it to customers in an effective manner. The scorecard of business is run by key performance indicators (KPIs) that demonstrate in numbers how you are ranking in the success, or failure, of your business.

Each business will have a different set of KPIs critical to their success, and you should not copy someone else's KPIs just because it seems like a good idea. For example, if you are in the business of distributing physical goods, you need to keep a close eye on your profit margin, making sure that you aren't losing money with every sale. If you sold $1 million worth of goods (revenue), but it cost you $1.1 million to buy your materials and run your business (cost of goods sold), you're left with a debt (loss) of $100,000. It doesn't matter if you increase your revenues if you are losing $0.10 on every dollar you gain in sales.

Don't let the numbers belong to the bean-counters. If the beans run out, you are out of business and nobody will care how great your idea was.

Here are the common KPIs that CEOs keep a close watch over each month, quarter, and year:

- gross revenue
- cash flow
- cash on hand
- gross margin
- profit margin
- customer growth
- growth of customer value
- lifetime value of a customer
- profitability by line of business
- staff turnover
- return on investment (ROI) on advertising
- prospect-to-customer conversion ratio
- staff utilization
- customer satisfaction
- customer retention

A lot of these numbers mean nothing if analyzed in isolation but mean a lot if you can trend them over time. If you were to put all of these KPIs in charts and tracked them over the past 2 years, you would easily see trends that could help you grow your business or spot problems before they become mission critical.

Become a Numbers Person

You may not be a numbers person, but as a business owner, you need to have regular KPI reports and watch them regularly to understand your business as a whole. I've recently joined a CEO group (CEO

Global Network) to help me gain a better hold of my KPIs and keep me accountable to growing the business. If you don't know where to start, I'd recommend you get counsel from an experienced CEO who has a great track record for managing KPIs in a growing business.

I regularly consult with business owners in an effort to help them grow their companies. The first thing I ask for is their financial statements because numbers don't lie. Numbers don't always predict what's in the future, but they certainly show what's happening right now. You might be shocked to hear that a good number of business owners I've come across would make more money flipping hamburgers than running their own businesses.

Make sure to find the right numbers to measure in your business (total volume of sales/gross revenue/repeat customers/monthly burn rate/lifetime customer value, etc.) and review them regularly — at least monthly. Don't wait until tax season to start preparing your financial reports.

Know Your Burn Rate

If you've never heard this term, you need to learn it. Your burn rate is how much cash your company will burn through each month just to stay in business. Add up all of your monthly expenses, including how much money you need to pay yourself to live. This total is your burn rate.

In the beginning, it's important to keep your burn rate low so you don't go under waiting for revenue (incoming cash). Revenue can be sparse in your first year of business, and once you run out of cash, it's game over.

It's helpful to break down your burn rate into a monthly, weekly, and even daily figure so that you can accurately measure against your revenue. If your burn rate is $550 per day and your incoming cash is only $400 per day, you know well before the end of the month that you're not going to make it. You'll either need to find extra revenue (sales) or quickly cut expenses to make sure you can get to the next month.

NUMBERS SHOW WHAT'S HAPPENING RIGHT NOW.

Don't Be Fooled

Some companies are a dog-and-pony show. They talk a big game but don't deliver. They may have 20,000 Facebook fans but be $2 million in debt with little annual revenue. Don't be fooled by competitors who try to distract you from things that matter. Innovation, customer satisfaction, and retention are real things to be proud of, not just "likes." Facebook doesn't send cheques out based on how popular you are; customers pay for your product.

If you visit the downtown core of a city, you'll notice a lot of nice cars — cars valued at triple or ten times an average annual salary — being driven around by various people. I remember coming to the realization in my 20s that not all of those people owned those expensive cars. Many people lease new cars that they can't afford to buy just because they like the way it makes them appear to other people. They are creating an illusion of success. The same is true of businesses.

Businesses can have the fanciest office, nicest website, or best booth at a trade show and be operating in pure debt. They look successful but could go bankrupt any day if they default on their loans. Don't be fooled by those people who parade around like industry leaders; they may be gone tomorrow.

Turn Success into Numbers

This chapter may seem boring, but understanding your finances is the hardest — and most important — part about running a startup. You may have a great idea, but if you can't pay your bills, you won't be able to get it to market.

To help you plan for a successful company, create a work-back plan that looks at the end goal. It's fairly simply to do.

For example, imagine you sold widgets at $100 each and you needed to sell 100 widgets per month to break even, or sell 200 widgets to have a successful company. Knowing that we want to sell 200 widgets each month, let's divide that into an average of 20 working days per month, meaning that we need to sell 10 widgets per day. Now find out how many sales calls you need to make to sell 10 widgets. If you only land 10% of deals from cold calls, you need to make 100 calls a day to sell 10 widgets.

So you need to make at least 100 calls a day to sell 10 widgets, and you need to sell around 200 widgets per month to have a successful business. You should now focus on how you can make these 100 calls and measure your success. I understand that nothing is guaranteed, but you need to plan for success and measure it along the way. Spend some time applying this work-back plan to other areas of your business so that you can see if your business is viable.

At Candybox, we create work-back plans every day for companies that are looking to generate leads online. It's a simple equation that helps companies determine how much money they need to spend to help their sales teams. Build formulas that work for your business and check your progress regularly.

Turn Numbers into Graphs

So you've billed your customers $50,000 last month. Is that good or bad? The short answer is: It depends.

If you regularly bill your customers $100,000 each month, then $50,000 is bad. If you have increased your billing by $10,000 each month from $0, and you're now at $50,000, that's good.

Staring at numbers is no one's cup of tea, which is why you need to look past your numbers into graphs. Take all of your critical data and put it into graphs that represent different areas of your company over time.

I have one big, ugly online Google sheet that contains all of the most important numbers I need to run my company. Everything from new sales to employee hiring projections to customer retention is on one sheet that has over 20 graphs. At any time, I can scroll through these graphs for a visual representation of what's going on in my company, which could be good, bad, or just ugly. It gives me a lot of answers on a regular basis, and instead of giving people my best guess when making major decisions, I can reference our real numbers and charts.

It's hard to visualize what's happening in your business when you are just looking at rows of plain numbers. Compare Figure 1 and Figure 2 on the next page. It's difficult to understand your sales growth at a glance in Figure 1, but Figure 2 provides a much clearer picture in less than a second.

By looking at Figure 2 you can see that sales were not growing until the end of July, but that since then you've been experiencing rapid growth. The thick black line shows you the overall revenue trend, which you can compare against each month. In the next year of business, you should plan to make up for your growth slump in the spring/summer, and plan to hire more people or get more materials in the fall.

FIGURE 1

ANNUAL SALES

Month	Sales
January	$10,000
February	$20,000
March	$30,000
April	$35,000
May	$41,000
June	$43,000
July	$39,900
August	$70,000
September	$84,000
October	$92,000
November	$110,000
December	$140,000

FIGURE 2

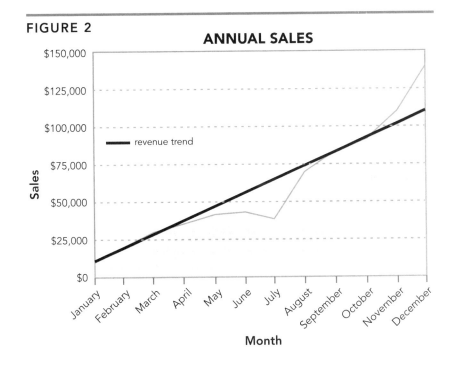

ANNUAL SALES

You may not need this in your first few months of business, but it's a habit to get into so you can manage your growth over time. You don't need expensive software, just a basic understanding of how your data can be plotted out in a spreadsheet. I personally prefer to use online spreadsheets so multiple people can feed me numbers in real time instead of having to transfer files across departments each week or month.

Don't be afraid of the numbers. Become a numbers wizard and make them work for you!

8

OWN
YOUR
CALENDAR

We all have the same amount of time each day. Success belongs to those who steward it wisely.

Everyone is busy. I've yet to meet a person who says they aren't. But some people treat their calendar like a prison that confines them every day, as though it were filled in by someone else. Stop complaining about being busy and decide how you want to spend your time.

I'm always busy, but it's my job to make sure I'm busy doing *the right things*. When I started my first company, I calculated that I needed to make $278 every workday. That was my revenue target to stay in the black. If someone asked me for my time and I couldn't make at least this amount of money, I would decline to do it.

"Darrell, can I get you to help with this project? It will only take you 1 day and I can pay you $200."

Many people who are just starting up would take this offer because they think any money is good money. But that's not true. If you accept this offer, you lose the *opportunity cost* of working on another project that can hit your goal. If you accept what is unacceptable, you accept a fate of future failure. Plain and simple.

"But, Darrell, don't you have the time to do this?"

No, I don't have the time to lose money. I need to win.

It's not that everything you do will produce revenue, but that should be the end goal. For example, going to a networking meeting, startup conference, or trade show isn't a guaranteed money-maker, but these kinds of events can help you reach your goal by growing your connections and business.

Set Boundaries

If you want to own your calendar, you first need to set boundaries for the things that you value in life. Want to keep a workout routine in the morning? Set your schedule around your workout. Want to stop working at 6 p.m.? Close your laptop at 6 p.m. It's that simple. Use your calendar to set boundaries on your workday and don't change it.

As a millennial, I've found that our generation has lost its grip on boundaries. When we send a text message, we expect a response within a few minutes, if not sooner. We check our phone notifications all the time, some of us while driving. We allow and even embrace interruptions instead of focusing on one thing at a time.

I'm constantly bombarded with distractions. I recognize that it's a challenge for me to stay on task for longer than 10 minutes at a time but that it's critical for my future. If I can't focus, I won't get anything done and will wonder why I haven't accomplished anything this year.

SET BOUNDARIES ON YOUR WORKDAY AND DON'T CHANGE THEM.

When I started my first company, I worked out of a closet. It was 5' x 4' and was upstairs by my kids' bedrooms. In order to be successful and put in a solid 8 hours of work per day I needed to set boundaries with my own family. The rule was that if my door was closed — albeit a closet door — daddy was unavailable. This might seem harsh when you consider that it might be my kids on the other side of the door, but if I couldn't manage my own schedule, I wouldn't be able to grow my new company. After 5 p.m., the door was opened and a different boundary was in place: Clients knew that I was offline and would not answer their calls and emails until the next day.

Recently I watched an interview with former president Barack Obama and Jerry Seinfeld. Obama spoke about his daily routine, how he gets up at 6 a.m. and completes a one-hour workout before his day begins. I was floored. Here you have a world leader waking up in the morning and running on a treadmill so that he can stay healthy. No phone calls, no texts, no emails. Just a man and a treadmill. I think we'd all be comfortable admitting that we aren't as important as the president of the United States. Nonetheless we somehow dupe ourselves into thinking that if we don't get back to that email or answer that text that the world is going to collapse. It's time to take a reality check, reassess our own self-importance, and set up some boundaries — and stick to them — like Obama.

Build vs. Manage

As the owner of your company, most of what you do during the day will fall into two categories: building your company or *managing your company*.

Typically, most of the emails you receive will fall under the *managing your company* category. Customers need help, employees need an answer, a bill needs to be paid — you are receiving an email because someone needs something from you.

Your personal task list of things you want to accomplish (your to-do list) resides in the *building your company* category. These are things that no one is asking you to do, but that you know need to get done in order to move your company forward.

In order to grow a company you need to balance both of these categories.

Focus too much on managing your company and you are only operating a business, not growing it. Months can go by without any meaningful growth because you are too focused on the daily grind and what customers are asking of you. If you get stuck here, you'll be managing your company until you retire and chances are it won't grow beyond you or a small team.

Focus too much on building your company and you may ignore and alienate your customers and staff. This happens when an entrepreneur is always looking toward the next step in their company without understanding their current commitments and operations. They move on too quickly without setting a good foundation for the company to run without them. If they try to build the next level in their business, their foundation may crack and the entire thing could come falling down.

A few years ago a major retailer entered Canada and immediately opened 200+ stores within the first year of business. It didn't take long for them to run out of cash and go under because of underperforming stores and logistical issues. Customers reported empty shelves, poorly assembled displays, and a lot of "coming soon" promises that were never realized. The retailer was too focused on working on the growth of their business rather than understanding the problems in their business, and they failed because of it. Don't fall into this trap.

Find Balance

You are the owner of your calendar so that means you need to prioritize both building and managing your business in your calendar. For my companies, I set goals to grow by 80% each year, and historically I have not hit these numbers. I've been able to grow by about 50% per year (year over year) for the past 6 years (earning a spot on *Maclean's* Growth 500 ranking of Canada's Fastest-Growing Companies in 2018). I could stay late, work weekends, or push harder in an effort to reach 80%, but I have boundaries in place to make sure that it doesn't take over every waking minute of my day.

I block off time in my calendar for creating growth strategies, and dedicate time to performing activities to ensure this happens.

Many people have asked me, "What are you doing to grow your company so much?" The answer is different every year. Sometimes it's pounding the phones and calling new customers. Sometimes it's building digital strategies to generate leads. Sometimes it's growing the team so we can handle the work and scope out new talent.

Take some time to identify the three activities you can do this year to grow your business and then work it into your calendar.

Use a Time-Saving App

I have no idea how people can manage their schedules in their head. It doesn't work. At least not for me. I have every 15 minutes mapped out in my calendar, and it's a smorgasbord of meetings, tasks, events, reminders, and lunches. I use Google Calendar to stay on top of everything, including reminders to eat lunch or else it just won't happen.

I also realized years ago that I was spending a ton of time booking meetings. Some email exchanges would go back and forth four or five times before a time was settled, which distracted me from doing important things (like the actual meetings themselves). To save this time, I pay about $9 per month for **calendly.com**, which allows me to send a link to others so that they can book a time that works for them. They can't book time that is already allocated (which is another reason why I need to put every task in my calendar), and once it's booked it will send them instructions on where I want to meet (phone/studio/online) and send reminders before the meeting happens. This tiny tool probably saves me sending and receiving about 400 emails every month.

Avoid Time-wasters

As you grow your company, everyone will want your time. As an owner you may even think that those people are entitled to it. This is very wrong. You control your time.

Every month, evaluate your work habits and find out where you are wasting time. Here are some things that people waste a ton of time on that I think can be eliminated:

Email: Learn how to control your inbox with rules, and stop trying to organize everything into folders. (I'll show you a better way in the next chapter.)

Go-nowhere customers: I don't know why, but some prospective customers out there will never become customers even though they love meeting with you. I'm not sure if they are lonely, bored, or just like doing lunch, but some people just waste your time. After you discover you are dealing with one of these people, let them know that you are too busy to meet or move them to a 15-minute call instead of a 2-hour lunch meeting.

Long meetings: Why do you need a 1-hour meeting when a 15-minute one will do? I've already covered this (see page 61), but it's critical: Stop wasting time shooting the breeze in these long pointless meetings that go nowhere fast.

Repetitive small tasks: Even though small tasks (getting the mail, tidying up the office) may take a few minutes, it's still something that takes your attention away from your main goal: running your company. Identify these tasks and delegate them quickly. I'm not saying that you are above any task — I have no problem taking out the trash when needed — but everything can't rely on you to get it done or you're in trouble.

Doing someone else's job: Did you hire someone to do something? Let them do it. Don't spend time micromanaging them (see page 113). You have better things to do. If you are spending 20 hours per month managing their 150-hour schedule, you've hired the wrong person or you haven't equipped them properly.

This list will change every year as your business grows, but it's important you keep assessing and reacting as your company grows so you can optimize and be master of your time.

9

AUTOMATION
HACKS

One of my favourite words is *automation.*

We live in an age where a few dollars per month can save you hours of repetitive tasks and time wasted. If something can save me one hour per month, I'm all ears. If you break everything down into a cost per hour, find out what one hour is worth (total revenue per month divided by 150 hours) and evaluate how much time that tool saves you. Now compare these numbers. If it saves you money, get it.

Here are a few of the tools that I use to automate my company. I'm not advertising for any of these companies — they haven't paid me to be in this book — I'm just sharing what works for me in hopes that they will help you. Since every business is different, you'll need to experiment to find what works for you.

Sales Hacks

GoToMeeting: Host online meetings instead of meeting clients in person. In real life there is no such thing as a

30-minute in-person meeting. You need to book at least 1 hour, and then factor in maybe 2 additional hours getting to and from that customer. By using this software you've just reduced a 3-hour venture into 30 minutes that you can slot between other meetings or activities.

Calendly: As mentioned earlier, this simple tool allows customers to easily book time in your calendar that you've delineated as available and automatically sends them instructions about the meeting. This software will save you from the back-and-forth of trying to find a time that works for both of you.

Viewedit: I hope this handy-dandy Chrome extension is still working and free when you are reading this book. It's not very popular, but I've been a super user for the past 12 months and it's completely changed the way I send emails to prospects and customers. This tool allows you to record your screen, along with a video of you (on your camera), and instantly embed it into an email. It's easy to use, free, and very effective for getting people's attention.

LinkedIn: I've tried to avoid talking about digital marketing in this book as my biases are clear, but this pertains to everyone in business. Simply by using the free version of LinkedIn properly, you can easily prospect and approach new customers using the advanced search function. If you want to learn more about this, I've created a free 30-day boot camp that anyone can sign up for here:

candyboxmarketing.com/linkedin. In 30 days, you'll be able to network like a pro on one of the largest business social media networks.

Pipedrive: There are volumes of books written about CRM (customer relationship management) tools and conferences that you can attend in any major city, but Pipedrive is a hidden gem in my life. I've tried over 15 CRMs in the past 10 years and none of them have ever come close to what Pipedrive has to offer. This software gives you one dashboard where you can see and interact with all of your active prospects in a sales funnel. It's built for the salesperson who needs to update their pipeline quickly and see what they need to do today. I'm such an advocate of Pipedrive that I even emailed them a testimonial to use on their website.

Operation Hacks

G Suite: This suite handles your enterprise emails (because having an @gmail.com account just won't do) plus a lot of other things. You can also manage all of your employee calendars, store/share files, and collaborate on documents in real time. I manage all of my company's KPIs (see page 68) using online spreadsheets that I couldn't live without. These are all mission critical technologies of a business, so don't give it over to your brother-friend-cousin-mailman to manage for you.

FreshBooks: This is very industry specific, but this service runs my companies' invoice/payment system in a breeze. You can automate regular invoices, accept credit cards, and send out payment reminders. I run millions of dollars through this slick system every year, and it only costs about $50 per month. It's money well spent.

Basecamp: We use this project management tool for both our customer and internal projects. It's a super simple way to collaborate with other users that incorporates task lists and file sharing.

TeamGantt: To help plan out large waterfall-style projects we use TeamGantt to collaborate on team scheduling. It helps us identify delivery times and meet project launch dates.

Slack: This is one of the best internal communication tools that I've ever used. It basically replaces emails, chatter, instant messaging, and phone calls. It has channels that you can join or leave based on your role in the company and keeps everyone in the know.

Payworks: Don't mess around with complex stuff like payroll deductions. Everyone at my company has a Payworks login, and they get paid and book off vacation time without the hassle of a payroll department.

Gmail: I've mentioned email a few times, but no program is really to my liking. I've spent years customizing my inbox to work for me, instead of me working for my inbox. Google "Gmail like a Ninja" and you'll find an article I wrote that explains my top tricks for how to manage email.

Keyboard shortcuts: I have so many shortcuts on my computer it's scary. If you find yourself typing out the same thing over and over again (like an invitation to book a meeting), you can use your computer's operating system to set up a keyboard stroke that will automatically insert a pre-set script. If I want to book a meeting with someone by email or text, all I need to type is "cal30" and it automatically inserts a paragraph of instructions and a link to book a 30-minute phone call. Snazzy.

Buy an Apple: Okay, I know that this may be offensive to some. I used to be a huge advocate of PCs and hated Macs. I finally switched because I realized I was spending about 30 minutes a day troubleshooting crap that wasn't working until I finally saw the light. I haven't restarted my computer in 6 months, and spend no time managing the crap on my computer.

I hope you find my list useful. Have other tools that you'd include? Shoot me an email at **darrell@candyboxmarketing.com**. I'd love to hear about them.

10

BUILD A VIRTUAL OFFICE

It's the dream: Work from anywhere, anytime, on any computer. You are now your own boss. The cuffs are off. The chain has been cut. It's glorious, it truly is. But it takes careful planning to live the dream, and not every business — or person — can do it.

Our journey from a virtual to a hybrid studio was a long one, but I made sure every step of the way that I wasn't building an office that I hated. When I worked in the corporate world, I hated the fact that I had to sit in a car for an hour a day just to sit in a cubicle and look busy. I hated the amount of clutter that surrounded the office, the never-ending emails people printed just so they could put it on their desk to remind themselves that they needed to deal with it. I hated the daily interruptions that I couldn't avoid of staff members asking questions. I hated that we had to work extremely hard just to cover the cost of our office and that a lot of our revenue was tied up in overhead.

Candybox Marketing was a virtual company for its first 6 years. I hired full-time staff who worked from home, and I personally worked from my home office, cottage, or local coffee shop. I love working virtually and enjoy offering this to as many team members as I can. It cuts down on overhead, management of the space, and logistics, and increases the time available to get things done. Even though we now have a studio space, we keep the virtual office alive by giving most of our team the option to work from home whenever it works best for them.

> If one of my employees feels sick, I don't want them spreading it to everyone in the office.

> If driving conditions are dangerous, there's no need to risk lives on the road.

> If someone is getting a furniture delivery, there's no need to take a vacation day.

I believe that if you create a work environment that's flexible for the team, everyone will be happier and healthier.

Set Ground Rules

My other agency, Launch48, required a physical space in which clients could come and build websites in a studio. Since the space we rented was local and close to where many of the employees had their virtual offices, I decided to let the team use that space to work in when they wanted, as we had extra workstations available.

I was surprised by what happened next: My staff, who enjoyed the camaraderie of being together, started working out of the studio more and more. We even attracted new talent who would not have applied if it was a work-from-home position. The employees loved the space and no longer wanted to work from home.

Since I didn't want to go into the office every day, I built a hybrid model for work. Here were the ground rules:

- The "office" was a workspace only. There would be no designated spots or desks that could be claimed.
- If you were in the studio, you wanted to be there. You didn't need to be there if you didn't want to be (applied to most team members).
- No clutter, paper, or crap allowed. No drawers. Just a place to work.
- All meetings would accommodate attendance both in person and virtually so that work-from-home staff wouldn't feel left out.

As soon as someone starts breaking these rules, they create the reason why I need to be in the studio, and our arrangement moves quickly from virtual to actual, so I make it very clear: The studio is a place for work, client meetings, or collaboration. You aren't doing me a favour by showing up.

So how do I manage a team that is *somewhat* virtual?

We use Slack and a few other apps to keep an eye on our progress. If we are working, Slack is on and we are available to one another. We also use other internal apps to measure time and progress on projects so that we can see how well we are using our time. Again, numbers don't lie, so poor performance is easily measured by a few helpful graphs instead of by attendance at the studio.

One of our core values at Candybox is honesty. I'm okay if people are sick or make mistakes, but they need to be honest with me. If I discover that people are taking advantage of the freedom that I've given them, it would be difficult for me to continue working with them, just as it would be in any other company.

If you can't trust that someone will work their designated hours, they are probably not the best candidate for a virtual office. Some people need to leave their homes and arrive at a different location in order to prepare mentally and start working, and that's okay. Virtual offices don't work for everybody.

If I'm interviewing someone for a virtual position, I ask a few pointed questions in an effort to understand what type of work environment they thrive in. For example:

> If you had the option to work at our office or work from home, which would you choose and why?
>
> Do you have a quiet space to work uninterrupted at home?
>
> Do you need regular interaction with staff members during the day to keep you happy?
>
> Have you ever worked from home before? If so, how did it go?
>
> Describe your ideal environment for getting a lot of work done. What's around you?

Asking questions like these will help you identify whether a person will succeed in or be hindered by a remote office. If you find out that someone needs to be around people every day to feel motivated, doesn't have a good track record working remotely, or has trouble focusing at home, you might not have the right environment for them even if they seem to be the right candidate.

Avoid the Pitfalls

Working in a virtual (or hybrid virtual) environment has a lot of advantages, but it also has some disadvantages that need to be mitigated. Here are examples of some that we've worked through over the past few years that you may find helpful.

> **Loneliness:** This is a very real thing. You live at home, you cook at home, you sleep at home, you relax at home … Holy crap, when do you ever leave home? We hold weekly 21-minute video meetings so that we can at least see each other every week, and we typically make the meeting more about people than tasks. We also encourage people to get out of the house on a regular basis to help fulfill their need for human interaction. We all need to make space for and welcome other people into our lives. I call this our "people tank." Some of us have very small tanks, and so can fill our tank simply by working from a coffee shop or library for a portion of the day. Other people have much larger tanks, and they need to be working alongside peers,

as well as have meeting spaces, whiteboard time, and open conversation. Find out how large people's tanks are and try to make sure that you can meet their needs, or they may become lonely and discouraged.

Physical strain: It's not easy working from home and sitting in a chair all day. Especially during winter months (we're Canadian), it can get very dark and depressing when you can't even go for a walk. Each winter, I remind everyone to get active in some way that works for them. From gym memberships to volleyball, we try to do something to keep the blood flowing.

It may seem like overstepping by encouraging people to do things in their time outside of work, but work is a large part of everyone's life. If your team is not happy with their work environment, they may want to leave. During the winter months I try to personally check in with every team member who is working remotely to make sure they are feeling good.

Workspaces: I always encourage any staff member who is new to working from home to set up a proper workspace and treat it as such. Don't be a couch lounger or kitchen-counter dweller. It starts to mess with you over time, and your family may not know when you are accessible and when you are not. In order to avoid distractions, I encourage people to find a quiet spot where they can work without being interrupted.

Live in the Cloud

One of my life goals is to live in the cloud. Okay, that sounds very nerdy, but it's true. Everything that I work on is stored in the cloud and most software that I use is web-based or a Chrome extension. This matters because if you have a virtual office, everything is on your computer. EVERYTHING. So if that computer falls into a pool, you're screwed. But if everything is stored in the cloud , you'll be fine!

Five years ago I accidently spilled an entire bottle of water on my laptop. I quickly flipped my laptop upside down so that the water wouldn't seep into the main computer and then put it in a shopping bag filled with rice. Great plan except you need to leave it there for 48 hours. 48 HOURS. I can't wait that long to get back to work so I grabbed one of my kids' 15" cloud laptops, signed in on Google Chrome, and was back in the game within 10 minutes. Emails got answered and files got sent. Business as usual.

Make it your goal to live in the cloud if you want to have a virtual company.

Embrace Flexible Workspaces

Your office space should work for your people, and no two teams are the same. I've come to realize that everyone likes to work differently so people need options. There isn't one kind of arrangement that will work for all companies, so stay flexible when you are planning out your workspace. You may have a team that's 80% virtual and 20% in-studio, or vice versa!

We have changed our workspace every year for the past 4 years and don't like to sign long leases for this very reason. Every time I think that we have created the best environment for our team, we get a few new team members who make different requests. Stay flexible and enjoy the journey!

11

BUILD
AN
A-TEAM

I love business books. I'm currently reading seven different business books (in audiobook and paperback) and can't get enough. If it talks about growth, I'm all over it and put it into practice right away.

One of my current favourites is *Good to Great* by Jim Collins. In it he says that building a company is all about finding amazing people and putting them in the right positions. If you can do this, you've got yourself a recipe for success, but failure to do this will burn out any new entrepreneur trying to get his product or service to market. I wholeheartedly agree.

A lot of entrepreneurs hinder their own growth because they are not able to, or are afraid to, build a team of people to push the company forward. Although this task is critical to building any kind of momentum, very few people are willing to risk taking on the overhead out of pure fear: *If I pay this person a salary, will I have enough to pay myself?*

The answer to this question is *yes* and *no*. Yes one month; maybe no the next. In my opinion, leaders are the last people who should benefit from the company. Staff should always be paid first — they have a contract with the business to make money, you don't. Plain and simple.

There have been months when I've not collected a salary from my own company because there wasn't enough in the bank or I opted to grow my staff instead. It's hard, it's depressing, but those are some of the pains of ownership. Again, running a company is not for everyone. If you can't live without a weekly paycheque, it's not the life for you. Adding people on payroll is a real pain that you need to face if you want to build something beyond yourself.

People Are Awesome

Entrepreneurs are awesome people, but they have limits. They may be good at some things, but not all things. That's the exciting part about adding people to your company: You start to fill in the gaps that you need to be successful.

One of the first real businesses I started was a design company that focused on print collateral and branding. The majority of our work was done in either Photoshop or Illustrator, but here's the kicker: I've never used either of these programs. I could learn how to edit an image in Photoshop or create a graphic in Illustrator, but I have no desire to do so.

I hired designers who were amazing at their jobs to get this work done so that I could focus on working *on the company* instead of working *in the company* (see page 38). If you know how to complete all of the things that your customers need, be forewarned: You may be tempted to do the work yourself and end up with a company that never grows.

Every time you hire someone, look for someone who adds a new skill set or expertise to your team. Don't look for someone like you; you already have you. When I was an IT manager, I met Brandon Lee, a successful entrepreneur who at that time owned *By Design Publishing,* a white-labelled home magazine that real-estate agents used to retain customers. He's now on his fifth company, and I consider him an expert at building successful teams. Brandon would always tell me to "find out what your weaknesses are, then hire those people who can fill in those gaps." Be like Brandon.

Over the past 10 years I've surrounded myself with some of the best marketing people in the industry and have had the privilege of being a part of their journey. It's all about finding awesome people.

Let Them Find You

If there's one thing that I look for in A-team members, it's people who already have a desire to work with me. I don't have all day to convince someone that they want to work for someone like me; they need to come with that already built in.

I make sure to put myself out there: to speak to college groups, blog regularly online, post on Instagram, and create awareness of my agencies' mission. If people are attracted to our purpose, mission, and vision, they are 80% there. All I need to do is a quick skill assessment and we have ourselves a winner.

IF NO ONE WANTS TO BE ON YOUR TEAM, IT'S NOT THEIR FAULT.

Recently my entire team wrote a blog about how they got hired at Candybox, and it was embarrassing to read because of how sporadic each hire was. But they all shared the same thread: They reached out and wanted to work for me.

Treat Your People Like Gold

If people are the most important part of a business, why do most companies treat their employees worse than their customers? Why do you see managers yelling at their team and seconds later answering the phone like angels? Business leaders who do this need to get their head checked.

I can count on one hand the number of times over a 10-year period that I've lost my cool with a team member, and I always followed up with an apology and an immediate change on my end. It's a CEO's job to support his team from behind, lead them from the front, and anticipate and shield them from problems that come up on all sides. It's not our job to be an arrogant front-facing leader who whips them from behind and fires them if they get out of line.

Treating your team like gold doesn't just mean that you pay them well — that's just good business practice. You need to treat them well in every area. Make sure they are taken care of in the workplace, ask them about their families, treat them to a lunch out, have fun with them. This can't be faked. You actually need to care about these people because there's nothing worse than empty empathy.

In my experience, most leaders run their companies based on fear. They make their staff afraid of being reprimanded, embarrassed, or even fired. They raise their voices during meetings and make people feel small and unimportant.

I often notice this the first few weeks after I hire someone who had been a manager elsewhere. They assume that I'm some short-fused bomb, and seem nervous about bringing up problems or questions. It takes a while for them to adjust to a kinder business culture, but they stick around because they're actually cared for.

A-Teams Need A-Leaders

If no one wants to be on your team, it's not their fault, it's yours. Awesome people know that their time is valuable, and they don't want to waste it being treated poorly. Their careers are more than hours and remuneration; they want to move forward as individuals into an awesome future.

I've witnessed companies large and small fall apart in weeks because of poor leadership. Since leadership has the power to influence entire companies or departments, it doesn't take long for one person to dismantle an entire organization.

Company culture is hard to build and easy to destroy. Make sure that you don't allow anyone to hijack your culture, even for a day. Leadership is about demonstrating the behaviours that you want to see in others, not demanding certain behaviours.

One time a former employee was spreading false rumours about the stability of my company to some members of my team. These rumours circulated over a few days, and a number of people came to me concerned about the business. It was a Friday afternoon, and I considered calling a team meeting to address these rumours head-on. I realized, however, that I was feeling too emotional about it and decided to take the weekend to think about how best to communicate with my staff. I spent the weekend building a presentation about our company's direction, complete with facts about our growth and stability. When Monday rolled around, instead of coming down hard on the rumours, I presented a strong, positive outlook about the company, which also served to dispel the rumours and get everyone on the same page.

If you can't control your emotions, you can destroy years of hard work with a 5-minute angry rant or phone call, an accusatory email, or simply a bad attitude.

Train Everyone

If you hire for fit (culture) above function, you'll need to make sure your team members know what they are doing and how they need to do it. No one comes 100% ready for their work, even if they have all of the skills. Your company should have its own values, which get carried through all communication, policy, and action.

For example, at Candybox, we have an internal rule: We don't make sh*t. I'm not a person who swears — it's just not my style — so this rule is seldom spoken aloud. But when it is, I mean it. Our agency doesn't make anything that looks bad, ugly, or poor quality.

It's something we discuss with new team members on day one, regardless of their position in the company.

Why do we do this?

It's to make sure that we all carry the same vision. If we all strive for beauty, our customers will experience it around every bend. If you walk into our studio, our desks are beautiful, our workspaces are streamlined, even the way that we hide our computer cords is a work of art. Everything matters. Everyone needs to be aboard the same train.

Create Intrapreneurs

No, that's not a typo. Intrapreneurship is a real thing and it's in the dictionary. Intrapreneurship is a lot like entrepreneurship, but it's focused on working within a company, not on a company.

Intrapreneurs calculate and take risks, come up with new ideas, and execute them with the team, but don't need to own or start the company. There are a lot of similar traits between entrepreneurs and intrapreneurs, but for some reason only entrepreneurs get attention.

Once you start a company, you'll need a few intrapreneurs to keep the growth alive. You need others in your team to see opportunities, solve problems, and take risks. If everything is dependent on you to see and execute, you've just limited your growth to your own abilities.

In order to create a culture of intrapreneurs, you need to establish an environment where intrapreneurs can thrive and feel supported. Here are a few things that I've seen over the years that can help grow a team of intrapreneurs:

Encourage risk: Say yes more than you say no. If you are always saying no to new ideas, people will stop giving them. When people ask me if they can take a risk on something, 9 out of 10 times I'll say the same thing: *Go for it!*

Embrace failure: If people feel that failure will count against them, they won't try. If one of my team members takes a risk and fails, we typically spend time discussing what could have been done better or differently and end it on a positive note. I always thank them for taking the risk.

Empower your team: Your team needs to have the power/authority to take risks, so give it to them. Give them a budget that they can play with or time to work on a growth project.

Remember that every interaction with your team, every meeting, and every email is an opportunity to build them up. Don't let the busyness of business keep you from growing the team that will take your company to the next level.

The Millennial Advantage

Every time I hear someone use the word "millennial," I throw up a little in my mouth. It's become synonymous with the image of lazy, entitled "snowflakes" who live in their parents' basements. But even though I hate the term, I love this generation — my generation.

Most online resources delineate millennials as the generation born between 1980 and 1995, and describe them as the first generation that grew up as technology natives. But it goes downhill from there. If you spend any time on social media, you'll be battered with articles discussing how millennials have ruined everything from golf course memberships to bread to the car industry. *The Washington Post* recently wrote an article about how millennials are opting for paper towels instead of napkins because of their convenience, cost, and practical use — so looks like we may be ruining the napkin industry, too.

For some reason, the media loves to hate us, but I truly believe that we are an incredible generation that will change this world for the better. I'm not just another snowflake. Here are five reasons why I think that millennials currently have an advantage over other generations.

1. Education Overkill

The baby boomers gave the millennials one major piece of advice throughout their childhood: get post-secondary education. "Go to university if you want to make something of your life" was heard over and over again around our family's dinner table. A lot of us were even discouraged from getting a diploma and instead directed to get a degree or higher. If you read most reports on the job market today, even degrees are no longer recognized as an advantage!

This guidance has led to the millennial generation becoming the most-educated generation in history. Most of us did it. We went to school. We racked up stupid amounts of student debt. We dedicated years of our lives to this pursuit.

The problem with this plan was that a lot of us didn't get what was promised at the end. If you graduated around or after 2008, there were very few entry-level jobs available, your degree didn't mean much to employers, and companies were downsizing. We were promised jobs if we went to school, but the market didn't deliver. The media now calls us "entitled" and says that we expect special treatment when we are looking for employment. Entitled? More like disappointed.

But all is not lost. We still have the education that we paid for. We still expanded our minds and skill sets in various industries. We committed to learning, and even though some of us may be working simple jobs, we have within us knowledge that can be leveraged at any time.

Having graduated with a diploma in marketing, I'm one of the least-educated people in my company in the eyes of the world, but I surround myself with incredible people. The individuals who apply for jobs within my company have amazing amounts of education that they are looking to put to use. If you are looking for talent to build your company, millennials have it.

2. Digital Natives

Growing up in the digital age of smartphones and high-speed internet, most millennials come standard with digital skills that are needed in the workplace. I know that it's not a guarantee, but most millennials can type fast, navigate software easily, and conduct their own research online without any training. Gone are the days when companies need

MILLENNIALS HAVE THE TALENT YOU NEED

to provide days of on-the-job training for computer skills necessary to navigate the complex systems that we'd be faced with using each day.

If a millennial encounters a problem that they are not sure how to solve, you don't need to send them back to a tech school for more training. They'll just search for the answer online and in seconds find videos, blogs, and other resources that they can access immediately instead of waiting for specific instructions from someone else.

I'm not saying that other generations don't know how to do this, or that other people haven't adapted to the new norms of using technology to assist them in their job. What I'm saying is that millennials come job-ready or are at least savvy enough to learn on the job without a ton of intervention.

3. 20 Is the New 50

The demographic of people who start new businesses has changed over the past two decades. It used to be successful business people in their 50s leaving successful careers to start a new company. Nowadays, you're considered an entrepreneurial late bloomer if you're starting your first company in your 30s.

Business startup programs are full of teenagers and 20-somethings budding with ideas and potential. Incubators are taking people right out of university and coaching them to start their companies in weeks, not months.

The world has accepted the new norm of people like Mark Zuckerberg in their 20s leading multi-billion-dollar companies onto the NYSE. Investors are throwing millions at young people with great ideas every day without hesitation.

When I started Candybox 10 years ago, my age was a barrier for many potential customers, and I was confronted a few times about the legitimacy of my company because of how young I looked. Thankfully these days are over, as people recognize the abilities of young people to lead very successful companies.

4. Purpose over Position

In my experience with fellow millennials, this generation is striving to make a difference in this world instead of just collecting a paycheque.

Millennials are said to care more about how their contributions at work add to the common goal of the company (and the world) than how their contributions will simply earn them a salary. Don't get me wrong, millennials care about getting paid and should be rewarded for their contributions, but their job personally means more than that. This is good news for companies that have a noble mission they wish to accomplish and bad news for people who want drones to work on a line. If you don't have a compelling mission, you may want to rethink your business plan so you attract the next generation.

If you are passionate about what you do, you'll find millennials come alongside you to join the cause. They don't mind putting in the extra effort if you can show them *why* they are doing it and the goal that you are all trying to reach.

5. Access to Everything

If you are a millennial starting up a business, you need to realize that you have more access to resources, people, and tools than any generation in history.

Want to get advice from an amazing CEO in your industry? Read his blog.

Want to get an education in a particular subject that you know nothing about? Take an online course.

Need help understanding how to register your business online (see Chapter 1)? Google it.

I don't think most millennials realize the privileges of being born in our era. We have access to more resources than any other generation, but many of us don't use it to our advantage.

If you are starting a business, most of what you need can be accessed online in seconds without almost any effort. We've been given the best tool to help us start our business, so what are you waiting for?

It's time for millennials to stop complaining about the issues that we've faced in our generation (poor media coverage and lack of corporate jobs) and start using our advantages for our benefit. I believe that every generation is going to be blamed for something, but that change is a good thing for those who understand how to adapt.

As a marketer, I'm able to serve my customers by using my knowledge as a millennial to understand how to reach other millennials with advertising. If you are a millennial entrepreneur, you'll be able to reach the new generation of buyers easier than your older counterparts who don't always understand how we communicate.

Millennials, let's show this world what we can do with all that we've been given.

12

MICRO-
MANAGEMENT
IS FOR
LOSERS

Micromanagement occurs when a manager closely observes and/or controls the work of his/her subordinates or employees.

No one wants to be a micromanager. No one will ever say, "I'm a great micromanager." It has a negative connotation, and people who micromanage typically don't know how to do any better. Here are things that you'll often see micromanagers do:

1. Spend more time watching their employees work than actually doing something productive.

   Micromanagers feel as though it's their job to watch people, which is technically more like babysitting than managing. Babysit people if you have babies, but if they are truly competent adults, then manage them.

2. Criticize the different ways people get their jobs done.

   Spend a few minutes watching another person navigate a computer and you'll quickly realize not everyone does things the same way. Just because a person completes a job differently than you do, doesn't mean that they are wrong or ineffective at the job. Let people do things their own way as long as the end product is good.

3. View their team members as below them instead of above them.

In my opinion, a great manager supports and grows their team. They are below their team, lifting them up to their highest potential. If you look at the way most people manage their teams, however, you often find it's the opposite. A micromanager's ego gets in the way of managing and the hierarchy has gotten to their head.

4. Take on all of the work themselves because no one does it right (or the right way).

Micromanagers may be very good at their job, but that doesn't mean they know how to manage others. Managers need to help, lead, and guide, not control others. If you spot someone taking work away from people, that manager likely has control issues and needs a lesson in management.

The funny thing is that many micromanagers who read this list won't admit to doing these things, but their actions give them away. Micromanagers are self-destructive entrepreneurs because as their company grows, they have to do more to keep up with the volume. They are the people who are working all hours of the night to get projects done instead of properly delegating tasks.

MANAGERS NEED TO HELP, LEAD, AND GUIDE, NOT CONTROL.

Whenever my company grows, I need new people to take tasks from my list and add it to theirs. Once the task is theirs, I'm done with it. I trust that it will get done properly. I only intervene if problems occur. If they can't do it properly, either I haven't trained them properly (which can be solved) or they aren't the right person for the job and someone else needs to manage it. You can't just take it back. That's not growth.

It Will Kill You

People think that micromanagement is bad because it's terrible for those being micromanaged. I think it's terrible because it can hurt your entire business, including the person micromanaging. If you micromanage your team, every new team member means a whole new set of responsibilities are added to your plate, which simply cannot scale. How can you ever expect to grow beyond 5 people if you need to be involved in every detail with every person? Imagine how large your workload will be once you reach 20 people or 50 people? What a nightmare.

Here are seven ways in which micromanagement kills business:

1. Micromanagement will kill your company culture: Everyone will feel like they are being treated as though they are dumb and incapable of making decisions.

2. Micromanagement will kill your business growth: Leadership spends all of their time managing details instead of growing the company.

3. Micromanagement will kill the potential for employees to take ownership over their different areas of the business: Leadership has assumed responsibility for everything.

4. Micromanagement will kill productivity: Employees get tired of redoing work the way leadership determines is right.

5. Micromanagement leaves everyone feeling frustrated: Good talent will walk out the door and look for new opportunities.

6. Micromanagement will hinder employees' abilities to develop problem-solving skills: People are told how to solve problems, not asked to solve them, and they end up feeling like their opinions don't matter and won't even try to solve problems.

7. Micromanagement will kill your schedule: Leadership needs to be around for every piece of work to be approved or shipped. They need to be present for the wheels of business to turn, and any time a leader is sick or absent, the company comes to a grinding halt.

If you want your business to grow, you'll need to evaluate these points regularly to make sure you aren't creating a business that will implode if it grows. No one sets out to micromanage a business, but anyone can develop these bad habits as a company grows.

Fight the Urge

If your business has a problem and you are the owner, it's natural to want to solve the problem yourself. If you didn't, it would show a lack of care for your business. But if you have hired someone to help you solve problems, it's critical to let them do their job.

If you take over someone else's job because they did it wrong, guess what? You have a much bigger problem on your hands that may take years to undo. How does this happen? Let me tell you a story about when I almost lost my crap.

Years ago I had a team member who was managing a large online campaign for a customer. The customer complained about a recent invoice, and after looking into it, we discovered that we spent $5,000 more than we should have on the campaign. The customer refused to pay the overage. I reviewed all of our communication and it was clear that the problem was on our end. Even though we weren't legally on the hook for the payment, in the interest of keeping this customer, I decided to eat the $5,000 cost myself and issue an apology for the mistake.

During this process everything in me was screaming to take control of this situation. I wanted to institute weekly reports of advertising spend, be cc'd on every email about campaign fees, and create a change order form for my staff. At this time in my business, I couldn't afford to lose $5,000, and I just did.

I would have been 100% justified to fly in and do all of the above. Instead, I took a long walk to cool down before speaking to my team or making a rash decision. Then I called the person responsible for losing the money and I asked them what they were going to do to resolve this going forward. I allowed them to own the problem and empowered them to decide on the appropriate course of action. They came up with three different solutions that we implemented and still use to this day, and this problem never happened again.

FORCE YOURSELF TO ONLY ASK QUESTIONS.

So what? What if I had implemented the solutions instead of my team member, would that have been such a big deal? The short answer is *yes*. It would have been devastating. If I solved the problem for them, it would communicate the following messages:

- I'm responsible for cleaning up your mess instead of you.
- If there is a problem, I don't believe you have the ability to solve it.
- You are unable to create systems to improve your job: I need to do that.
- If you ever make a mistake, I will remove that part of your job.
- People aren't allowed to make mistakes.

All of these messages would have ripped into this person's confidence. I would have been left with an employee who depended on me to fix everything. That's an unscalable nightmare. Fight against the urge to fix other people's problems within your own company.

How can you do this? Whenever you are told of a problem, resist the urge to solve it or propose different solutions. Force yourself to only ask questions. Here are some of my favourites:

- That sounds like a big problem. What do you think is the best solution?
- What would you recommend as the best course of action?
- Or very simply: What are we going to do?

If a team member cannot solve the problem by themselves, you can offer two or three different options and ask them to choose the best solution. By approaching it this way, your team will feel empowered to solve problems on their own and will own the solutions for the long term.

True Macromanagement

If micromanagement is evil, you might think that macromanagement is the answer. It can be, depending on your definition.

Instead of being very involved, some managers don't get involved at all, which can end up being worse than micromanaging. If you leave people completely alone and ask them to solve everything by themselves, you risk alienating your staff. That isn't good leadership; it's absent leadership.

I'M ALWAYS BUSY, BUT I'M ALWAYS AVAILABLE.

If you want to manage people from afar, you need to institute ways that they can access you easily and without threat of punishment. I personally believe in having a "door is always open" policy by not having a door. I work alongside all of my employees so they know that I'm approachable. I'm always busy, but I'm always available.

Macromanagement means that you empower people to make their own decisions and don't punish them if they make the wrong ones.

But what if they make bad decisions? Well, that means that you haven't trained them well enough. If people can't make good decisions on a regular basis, it's a failure in your abilities to help them make the kinds of decisions that you'd make. This takes time and effort — the opposite of leaving people alone.

Macromanagement means letting others deal with the day-to-day, but having regular checkpoints to review progress, performance, and problems.

Annual or semi-annual reviews don't cut it. The gaps between check-ins are just too large if you are a growing company. I personally check in with all team members (or at least managers) once a quarter to make sure that I'm supporting them in their role. This isn't a time where I only tell them what I think about their role; it's my chance to ask questions. When you are not in the details, it's important to have regular meetings so that people don't stray from the company's vision, values, or focus.

Build Awesome Jobs

Want to retain your best people? Give them awesome jobs. No one leaves an awesome job where they are appreciated, empowered, and led. People leave jobs because they are mismanaged, abused, or unappreciated.

Companies spend hours trying to hire and retain the right talent using headhunters and agencies when that time would be better spent building jobs that people actually want. It's time to stop blaming people for not performing and look at what you're asking people to do and how they need to do it.

When I first started out, I hired a bookkeeper to work out of my home and organize my financials. This very talented bookkeeper quit after the first day. At first I was disappointed in her rash decision to leave so quickly, but after a few weeks I realized that I didn't set up a great work environment for her to work in. I failed and would never make the same mistake again.

Building an awesome job means that you think about every aspect of the position, including work environment, salary, benefits, culture, management, opportunity for growth … the list goes on. Creating a job is more than establishing an employee's responsibilities and salary. People want to be a part of something special. If you aren't creating that, you won't attract amazing people.

The Hard Truth

But what if this doesn't work? What if you train people well, give them your time, give them freedom, and they continue to fail over and over again?

This is a hard truth that I've learned over time: Building a team requires you to trust people, and people are bound to let you down at some point.

If someone is not performing in your organization, they're simply not the right fit. They probably don't have a future with your company, and this won't work for either of you.

Be slow to hire and quick to let go.

If someone doesn't work out at my company, I've hired the wrong person. It happens from time to time, but I'm at a point where I can typically tell in the first few days instead of waiting months to see the result. This is why offering probationary periods for new employees is so critical: It gives you time to evaluate the candidate during a trial period. If they can't succeed in 90 days, giving them another 90 days will most likely be a waste of time.

Keeping a warm body for the sake of getting something halfway done is not a recipe for success. Don't let your ego get in the way of letting go of the same employee you thought was going to be stellar.

For those employees who choose to leave your company, be sure to listen to them and gather intel for next time. Conduct an exit survey, capture their insights, and have a real conversation with them so that you can learn and grow and ask the right questions next time.

13

MANAGE STUPID GROWTH

I hope that stupid growth is part of your future. It's something that I love to see in any business. It's what gets me up in the morning. It's the Stanley Cup of the business arena.

In the book *Scaling Up*, Verne Harnish calls any company that grows 20% in top line revenue every year for 5 years in a row a "gazelle." Candybox has experienced about 50% growth every year for the last 5 years straight (Go Team!), which recently earned us a spot on *Maclean's* Growth 500 ranking of Canada's Fastest-Growing Companies (previously called PROFIT 500). That's stupid growth.

So as you can see, I've seen first-hand what stupid growth can do to a company, and I can tell you that it's not easy. From cash flow to acquiring talent, growth is seldom spoken about in a negative light, but it's a small business killer if you don't manage it properly. This chapter outlines some of the things that I've learned through the joys and sorrows of stupid growth.

Set BHAGs

During my first 4 years of business I was in survival mode. My goal was to get by, pay the bills, and hopefully grow along the way. I was a two- to three-person company for those first few years and didn't see any major growth. Although it was my hope to grow, I did not actively plan for it. It was only after I started setting regular goals that I noticed my actions changing to reflect the direction I had communicated to my team.

During this time, while I was running Candybox Marketing, I had also (unsuccessfully) started another company for launching SaaS product. It was called Social Stage, and I had three partners. That company lasted about a year and ended up going under because a change in Facebook's Company Page settings blindsided us. Afterwards I realized that I needed to either push Candybox to the next level or be okay with mediocrity. The following year I heard the acronym BHAG and it honestly changed my life.

The term Big Hairy Audacious Goals (BHAG) was first coined in 1994 by Jim Collins and Jerry Porras in their book *Built to Last: Successful Habits of Visionary Companies*. BHAGs aren't your typical goals. They're larger than life, strategic in nature, and emotionally appealing to anyone who hears them. I personally believe that nothing amazing is ever accomplished without first setting a goal.

Setting goals ensures that you never become comfortable with what you've achieved and challenges you to go beyond your comfort zone. Companies that don't have big goals are fatalistic and will accept whatever comes their way. What a sad way to exist.

BHAGs aren't wishful thinking. If you take them seriously, you'll figure out a way to achieve them. I break down all of my goals into tangible results so that each month I know whether I'm closer to my goal or if I'm missing it completely. I allow the pain of not reaching my goals to be in my face every morning so that it changes how I prioritize my day for growth.

Most years I start off with a BHAG that looks something like this:

I will grow revenues by 80% by December.

Every December I review what I've achieved throughout the year and establish a new goal for the next year. I make sure the goal is stupidly big, crazy in nature, and focused on growth. Then I break it down into monthly goals (which all contribute toward my annual goal) and set up goals for each department so that I can track my BHAG every single month. I print them out at home and put them above my desk where I can see them whenever I'm there working. Those monthly goals stare me in the face every single day to remind me what I'm doing. It's challenging to wake up to every day, but it keeps me focused.

Make It a SWOTA

When I took marketing in school, I learned how to create a SWOT analysis, which involves documenting a company's strengths, weaknesses, opportunities, and threats.

Strengths and weaknesses are things that the company has internally, and can typically be controlled by you. An example of a strength might be low prices, and a weakness might be customer service. You can control both items and they are a part of your everyday operation.

Opportunities and threats are things within your company's environment, but you cannot control them. Examples include environmental factors, political changes, your competitors, or even changes in technology.

Evaluating these four things will help you get a good handle on your company's position, along with any upcoming opportunities and threats. It's the 50,000-foot view of a company and its surroundings, and should be reviewed every quarter if you're going to be competitive in your marketplace.

A SWOT analysis will only tell you what's happening now; it doesn't have the power to move you forward.

Every quarter, my team walks through an internal company SWOT, but we have a little addition that makes this meeting worth our time. We finish up every session going over our action items based on reviewing the SWOT, making it our SWOTA.

Once you've defined your SWOT, you need your action items to accomplish the following:

1. Reinforce your strengths as a company and make sure that you don't lose your advantage.

2. Eliminate your weaknesses as a team with creative problem solving. Turn your weaknesses into strengths. Do you suck at delivering on time? Find out why and solve the problem.

Don't allow these to remain acceptable weaknesses for your next meeting.

3. Go after opportunities aggressively. If a major opportunity is coming up, put someone in charge of tackling that opportunity and give it a timeline. Don't get into the details of *how* it's going to be done, just empower someone to take it on.

4. Eliminate or mitigate your threats. Change what you do so that these threats won't take your company down. If it's an imminent threat, pivot, fight, strike back, or plan your exit. Don't just pretend it doesn't exist.

It's critical to involve your entire staff in these meetings so you can tackle the SWOTA together as a team. Remember, you can't solve everything in your company by yourself.

Pivot

As an entrepreneur, every day is going to look different (hopefully). In the beginning, you may be taking on a laundry list of tasks from sales to operations to admin and everything in between. You need to make sure that things get done, and this may include bank runs to deposit cheques, buying office furniture, calling customers to receive payment, and tons of other tasks.

No job is below you, but you need to make sure that every month you're pivoting your own schedule to take into account your growth. If every month is the same, you are maintaining, not growing. Your job description needs to change all the time to deal with stupid growth or you'll become the bottleneck in your business and prevent the company from growing any further.

HAVE A SOLID PLAN TO FIND YOUR NEXT HIRES.

You'll need a team of patient people to deal with your ever-changing roles within the company, and it's critical to communicate this to your team so they can understand why you are passing off tasks and prioritizing constantly. Be a professional pivoter.

Delegate Daily

Delegation is easier said than done. It's easy to delegate jobs that you can't do, but it becomes harder to delegate jobs that you can do or, even worse, you love doing. If you don't delegate, you'll limit your growth and will once again suffocate the business due to your inability to pass things off properly.

Truth: It takes more time to delegate a task than to do it yourself. I'm a father of four, and let me tell you how painful it is to watch my kids load the dishwasher. It's all wrong. For some reason I expect them to understand the system that I've perfected over years of trial and error and do it perfectly every time. It is so much easier to grab the stuff and load it myself, but that's wrong. I can't do their dishes forever, and I need to let them learn these tasks or I'll always be stuck cleaning up their mess.

Delegation does not mean that you throw your busy schedule at someone and expect them to pick it up right away. Delegation is best completed *when you are not busy* so you have the time to answer questions and assist with the first few attempts.

Plan Your Next Hires

When a company starts radically growing, leaders have a natural tendency to focus on the incoming work instead of the team that should be getting the work done. As a leader, you should be focused on (or delegating) the acquisition of your next few hires. You can't double your company in a year if you need to double your workforce and don't have these people ready.

My biggest regret in my early years of running a company was not hiring enough people. I scraped by with a few people and made it work, but I didn't have enough people to help grow the business. As a business owner, I would see how busy my team was, and would slow down sales by turning down new opportunities. If I'd had the bandwidth available, I would have grown the business more aggressively, but I had no plan to grow the team.

Make sure you have a solid plan in place to find your next hires. Map out what your organization chart would realistically look like if your business doubled tomorrow. Do you need more managers, more production people, or more salespeople? Figure that out now, and start mining for talent.

Say No

Saying no is one of the most powerful things that a leader can do when growing their business. I've accepted new lines of work that didn't match our skill set in order to keep growing the business, only to have it stress out my operations team as they tried to fulfill project commitments that were beyond their typical projects. I'm not saying that you shouldn't stretch your team with new requirements, but some projects are going to take more time than expected and won't get you closer to your own goal. Say no to projects that take your eye off of your BHAGs.

Make It a Team Sport

I'm not a fan of the way society praises the entrepreneur. Praising just the entrepreneur fails to recognize all of the people it took to make that one person succeed. I'm only where I am today because I have an incredible team, a supportive wife, encouraging friends, and a network of helpful business leaders who are willing to give me advice when I call them.

I love asking seasoned CEOs for advice. Not just because they know it all, but because they have a wealth of knowledge they usually love to share with others. You don't need to agree with, or do what they say, just consider their opinion. Join a CEO group or a local board of trade, and rub shoulders with people who have earned their stripes. One piece of advice could save you years of pain.

Every business owner needs to have a list of other CEOs, peers, or subject-matter experts that they can call on for advice in different areas. Not one person will have the entire picture, but collectively they can help you solve problems that are beyond your ability to solve. Personally, I have different people to call

SAYING NO IS ONE OF THE MOST POWERFUL THINGS A LEADER CAN DO.

on in each of the following areas (in no particular order): personnel, business models, innovation, human resources, charitable giving, taxes, legal issues, family life, spiritual life, and leadership. You need to have people in your corner who care enough about you to give you 10 minutes out of their busy schedule to work through a problem.

Go ahead and make a list of the different people that you know who can help you. Beside their name write the areas in which they specialize. Don't expect someone who gives you tax advice to also understand how to hire the next leader. Everyone is good at something, but nobody is good at everything.

Embrace Regular Dialogue

You can never communicate enough with your team. Don't have long, drawn-out meetings that go nowhere, but pick up your freakin' phone every day and talk with the people in your company.

As mentioned earlier, when you are growing quickly, everything needs to change. Obviously you need to be able to handle this

TALK
WITH THE PEOPLE IN YOUR COMPANY.

change, but if you are the only one who understands the full picture — your past, present, and where you are going — you need to recognize that not everyone else in your company will see the same picture.

Although I try to communicate with my staff all the time, it's an area in which I've failed time and time again. I'll make a change but then fail to thoroughly communicate it to all team members. The problem here is that their perspective of change will likely be different than mine. Some people don't like change. Some people are afraid of change. Some people won't understand why things need to change. Some people crave change. Making a change without having your team on board means that you may lose people or alienate team members because they don't understand what is actually going on.

If you are the type of leader who regularly tells people about where you are going, you may need to pull back on what you say if you aren't ready to deal with the consequences. If you throw something out there about the company's future, you need to understand that people will run through all of the scenarios of what that *could* mean for them and their job. It can cause unnecessary stress.

When your company is growing, make sure you dialogue about upcoming changes before they happen, dialogue when it happens, and dialogue after it happens. You'll notice that I'm using the term "dialogue" instead of "tell" — there's a big difference.

If you *tell* your team what's happening, you're not inviting them to contribute, challenge, or discuss the upcoming changes. If you *dialogue* with your team, you are having a conversation about their thoughts, feelings, and concerns about the changes.

Your team knows changes are going to affect your company, and they need to make sure they are ready. Don't think that you already know how it's going to impact them or their department. Ask them open-ended questions and let them help you with the change.

14

GET
STARTED

The most precious commodity new entrepreneurs have is their time, not their finances. When I reflect back on my first 10 years of building a company, I realize that I spent more time trying to build the business without realizing that I needed to build myself. This resulted in years of mistakes, small-thinking, and wasted time.

Sure, these same lessons can be learned over time, but most of us don't have the luxury of being able to spend 5 years with poor financial management to learn about cash flow. It would be much better to spend a week learning it from industry experts rather than slowly go bankrupt.

You are your greatest asset, but it's hard to acknowledge that you are also your biggest problem. You may make mistakes, you may be inexperienced, you may have fundamental personal flaws, you may suck at running a business — these problems will be magnified when you start and grow a business. If you're terrible at managing your own finances, imagine being in charge of millions of dollars. People think that money can solve all problems, but seasoned CEOs will tell you that the mistakes just become bigger.

I may sound terribly negative, but I regularly tell the people I work with that I'm the biggest problem in my business. Not the market conditions, poorly performing employees, or difficult customers: I am the problem. I own it 100%. This helps me push myself to grow even if it's uncomfortable, challenging, or painful. I believe that if I grow as a person, my company will follow. Poor leadership can never lead people beyond what they have achieved. If I want my team to go further, I need look no further than my own shortcomings to see what stands in our way.

Double Down

Want to invest in yourself? Double down your investment. Read books by business leaders you respect, read blogs by industry experts, listen to the audiobook biographies of successful entrepreneurs. Want to break into a new country or culture? Learn the language in your car while driving between meetings. Don't have connections? Spend one hour every day on LinkedIn sending personal notes to industry leaders.

We live in an age where information is just a click away, but that doesn't mean anything unless you plan to consume these amazing resources. It's unbelievable that we can now access entire university curriculums online for no cost and yet so many people say that they are limited by their education. We need to stop making excuses and start making a plan to invest in ourselves.

Be Ruthless

I was speaking with my friend Brandon Lee, and he asked me about my workout schedule. I told him that between running a business and having four kids I didn't have time to work out. Seems like a pretty good reason if you ask me, but his response will stick with me forever: "Everyone has time. You just haven't made it a priority."

Ouch. He was right. Of course I have time to work out, but I've prioritized other things above exercise and lied to myself that it was impossible to do. I could work less, sleep less, or relax less and prioritize my physical health, but I don't.

Ever since that day, when people talk to me about my physical activity, I tell them that it's not a priority so I don't continue to lie to myself. Be ruthless with yourself. If you aren't doing something, stop making excuses and just admit that you haven't made it a priority.

Be Brave

Throughout this book you've probably realized that starting and growing a business is no small feat. It's not for everyone, and no one who starts a business has it all together. I started with the dream of having a steady income to pay my monthly mortgage and monthly expenses. At that point in my life, that was brave.

Don't listen to the people who tell you how many businesses fail in the first 5 years. Instead, listen to the people who run successful companies because they took the risk. Every person, business, and idea is unique. Your entrepreneurial journey is going to look different from everyone else's. It's your time to take this crazy uncharted route and make things happen.

Launch NOW

The time really is now. Launching a company is becoming easier, not harder, every passing year. The cost of starting a business continues to decrease, and most people can do it out of their own home. Stop making excuses about why you can't start, and register that business today. If you miss your opportunity, you could be losing millions of dollars and a bright future. Most people spend 45 to 55 years of their life working so why not make every single day count?

Starting and growing a business is one of the most fun things I've ever done, and helping others do the same has become a personal passion of mine. Although I'm still learning a ton about building businesses, I hope you'll be able to glean something from my experience as a millennial entrepreneur who had to figure it out one day at a time.

With 10 years of startup under my belt, I understand why a lot of people who go it alone don't make it. There are tons of obstacles to overcome before you can even begin. However, I believe that if you take the time to learn how to overcome the most common roadblocks and hurdles, you can become the business leader of tomorrow. When

I started, I truly had no idea what it was going to take to build a company, but I met every day with persistence and the simple belief that I could make it work. Losing was not an option, so if something didn't work, it had to change.

Take a leap of faith in yourself, try something new, and then build and grow something awesome for the world to see.

Oh, and *pick up your freakin' phone!*

THANK YOU

Since this book tells much of my journey as an entrepreneur, I find it fitting to thank all of the people who played such a big part in my success over the last 10 years, along with the people who helped me make this book.

No part of my journey could ever have been accomplished without the unwavering and overwhelming support of my best friend, biggest fan, and wife, Tammy. Tammy played an integral role in my original decision to start Candybox and continues to encourage me through the good and bad times of learning how to grow a company. She had a lot of reasons to doubt me along the way but never once gave up on our dream. I'm eternally grateful for you, Tams.

To my kids, who give me space to work when I'm at home or tackle me when I walk through the door. I truly hope this book will help you in your future. I see you all as entrepreneurs in your own right, and I'll always be your biggest fan.

To my team (past and present) at Candybox. You are the best team that I could ever hope for. You have all individually contributed to this book in some way, and put up with my shenanigans on a weekly basis. Entrepreneurship is a team sport, but typically only the leaders get recognized. Everything that we've built has been due to your hard work and commitment to excellence. Thank you for putting your trust in me, and I look forward to continuing to grow together.

To my good friend Brandon Lee, who has been a wealth of knowledge during our shared entrepreneurial journeys over the last 10 years. Your pioneering spirit, passion for building teams, and experience growing companies has always been a huge encouragement to me.

To all of the faculty at Sheridan College who helped shape my thoughts about marketing, along with many of the students who now work alongside me. You have been an invaluable resource to me. More than half of my company consists of Sheridan College grads. You produce truly incredible minds.

To my entire book-launching team, including Mahfuz Chowdhury, Heather From, Ben Reimer, Tracy Bordian, Rob Scanlan, Eleanor Gasparik, and Karen Hunter. Thank you for all that you've done to get this out the door.

ABOUT THE AUTHOR

Darrell Keezer is a much sought-after author and speaker, and the founder of Candybox Marketing, a digital marketing agency based in Toronto, Ontario. Candybox is a recognized leader in launching innovative digital marketing campaigns and has a broad and influential client base in Canada and the United States. In 2018, Candybox was recognized on *Maclean's* Growth 500 ranking of Canada's Fastest-Growing Companies for "demonstrating foresight, innovation, and smart management" (Deborah Aarts, Growth 500 program manager).

Darrell was inducted into Sheridan College's Business Hall of Fame for his work in building an award-winning agency. He has also been named Entrepreneur of the Year by two organizations, and has won two Awards of Excellence in Business from the Governor General of Canada.

This is Darrell's second book. His first book, *37 Ways Your Website Died—And How to Resurrect It,* was published in 2014.

Darrell lives in Mississauga, ON, with his wife and four children.

INDEX